I0213440

A Theatrical Feast in Paris

Other books by Elizabeth Sharland

Love From Shakespeare to Coward

From Shakespeare to Coward

The British on Broadway

A Theatrical Feast in London

A Theatrical Feast in New York

The Best Actress (novel)www. sharland. com

A Theatrical Feast in Paris

✦

From Molière to Deneuve

Elizabeth Sharland

iUniverse, Inc.
New York Lincoln Shanghai

A Theatrical Feast in Paris
From Molière to Deneuve

Copyright © 2006 by Elizabeth Sharland

All rights reserved. No part of this book may be used or reproduced by any means, graphic, electronic, or mechanical, including photocopying, recording, taping or by any information storage retrieval system without the written permission of the publisher except in the case of brief quotations embodied in critical articles and reviews.

iUniverse books may be ordered through booksellers or by contacting:

iUniverse
2021 Pine Lake Road, Suite 100
Lincoln, NE 68512
www.iuniverse.com
1-800-Authors (1-800-288-4677)

ISBN-13: 978-0-595-37451-9 (pbk)
ISBN-13: 978-0-595-67502-9 (cloth)
ISBN-13: 978-0-595-81844-0 (ebk)
ISBN-10: 0-595-37451-4 (pbk)
ISBN-10: 0-595-67502-6 (cloth)
ISBN-10: 0-595-81844-7 (ebk)

Printed in the United States of America

This book is dedicated to

Diane Coles

Contents

ACKNOWLEDGEMENTS

Sheridan Morley, Hélène Catsiapis for the chapter on Noël Coward, the Noël Coward Society, John Money, David Sedaris, Adam Gopnick, Celia Cologne, Geoffrey Skinner, Didier Boidin and Martial Hamon at the InterContinental Hôtel, Paris, Stuart Foster, Colman Jones, and my husband Gerald.

Every effort has been made to trace all copyright holders, but if any have been inadvertently been overlooked, the author and publishers will be pleased to make the necessary arrangements at the first opportunity.

FAMOUS QUOTES

One cannot think well, love well, sleep well, if one has not dined well.

—Virginia Woolf

Only dull people are brilliant at breakfast.

—Oscar Wilde, An Ideal Husband

Those who do not enjoy eating seldom have much capacity for enjoyment of any sort.

—Charles Willliam Elliott, A Happy Life

A good cook is like a sorcerer who dispenses happiness.

—Elsa Schiaparelli

No mean woman can cook well, for it calls for a light hand, a generous spirit and a large heart.

—Paul Gaugin

Every night should have its own menu.

—Balzac

Beware of young women who love neither wine nor truffles nor cheese nor music.

—Colette

I never worry about diets. The only carrots that interest me are the number you get in a diamond.

—Mae West

Making love without love is like trying to make a soufflé without eggs.

—Simone Beck

Every fruit has its secret.

—D. H. Lawrence

In water one sees one's own face, but in wine one beholds the heart of another.

—French Proverb

There comes a time in every woman's life when the only thing that helps is a glass of champagne.

—Bette Davis, Old Acquaintance

We may live without friends, we may live without books, but civilized man cannot live without cooks.

—Owen Meredith

One should eat to live and not live to eat.

—Molière, L'Avare

Heaven sends us good meat, but the Devil sends cooks.

—David Garrick

That all softening, overpowering knell
The tocsin of the soul—the dinner bell

—Lord Byron

Some day you'll eat a pork chop, Joey, and then God help all women.

—Mrs Patrick Campbell to Bernard Shaw

This piece of cod passes all understanding

—Sir Edward Lutyens

Fame is at best an unperforming cheat;
But 'tis substantial happiness to eat.

—Alexander Pope

There is no love sincerer than the love of food.

—George Bernard Shaw

At dinner one should eat wisely but not too well, and talk well, but not too wisely.

—Somerset Maugham

The cook was a good cook, as cooks go, and as good cooks go, she went.

—Saki

Most dear actors, eat no onions or garlic, for we are to utter sweet breath.

—Shakespeare, A Midsummer Night's Dream

A bad liver is to a Frenchman what a nervous breakdown is to an American. Everybody has had one and everyone wants to talk about it.

—Art Buchwald

"You, who have ever been to Paris, know;
And you who have not been to Paris—go!

—John Ruskin 1835

PREFACE

Now that the Comédie-Française has announced that there will be English subtitles installed for some performances, a huge new audience of English speaking thespians will be coming to Paris with a renewed interest in the "House of Molière," as the theatre is known. The pleasure of now seeing and understanding their brilliant productions should stimulate the appetite to learn more about French actors, playwrights and directors who shaped the history of the their theatre from Molière to the present day.

It is interesting to try and compare their achievements with that of our contemporary performers and writers. The fact that some people may argue with me about George Sand being France's greatest woman playwright is a case in point. Her plays may be forgotten, but not her life and work. There have been other great French women writers, such as Marguerite de Navarre, Madame de Sevigne, and Marguerite Duras, and many of them achieved fame but they did not have four plays running simultaneously in Paris as well as notoriety as a novelist, as George Sand had. . Francoise Sagan wrote plays, and Yasmina Reza still does, but it is only the test of time to see what names survive, and become legends. The same comparison stretches still today when we watch actors either in the theatre or on film and wonder who will be remembered in 100 years time. When you read about Molière and Victor Hugo you wonder who could be compared to them today.

Molière's plays in turn inspired the budding novelist George Sand to write plays, two of which Sarah Bernhardt starred successfully in. The Comédie-Française played a great part in the careers of Molière, Sand and Bernhardt and for the first time, the plays will be available in English so that thousands of people can appreciate their work.

George Sand, then in her sixties, wrote to the young actress to thank her for performing like an angel, and a warm friendship developed between the two strong-willed woman. Bernhardt greatly admired the famous authoress, who defied convention by wearing men's clothes, smoking cigars, advocating and practicing free love. Talking with Madame Sand as the writer sat in her dressing room smoking or strolling with her in the Luxembourg Gardens, Bernhardt confided her ambition to be the greatest actress in the world.

One of Sarah's leading men was Lucien Guitry, who was then the most popular actor in France, and the father of Sacha Guitry. Sacha wrote two plays for Sarah although he beat out Sand by writing over 100 plays...however she wrote over 100 novels. Sacha Guitry in turn ran his own theatre company as did Bernhardt and he discovered brilliant french actors, including Michel Serrault and Jean Poiret.

The banquet room in the Grand Hôtel (see front cover) was the scene of one of Sarah Bernhardt's greatest triumphs. From a report by Joanna Richardson 'she wafted toward us in a halo of glory". It was on December 9th 1896 when a group of writers and actors planned a day of 'glorification" to honor her for her contributions to the world of theatre.

Dame Sybil Thorndike was the much loved leading actress in England for years during the middle part of the 20th Century, and now Dame Judi Dench is following in her footstep—but Sarah Bernhardt must remain the best loved actress in French theatre. Dame Judi Dench possesses the same kind of brilliance, discipline and love for the theatre as Sarah Bernhardt had. She toured the world, as has Dame Judi and her greatest achievements were playing the all the classical roles in Shakespeare. However it is interesting to note, that Bernhardt's huge successes in London were not only widely acclaimed, playing to packed houses but also all the plays were presented in French. There were no subtitles in those days so one has to wonder how she managed to convey her great gifts and whether some of her brilliant characterizations and subtleties as an actress could have been lost. It doesn't appear to be so, which is remarkable.

The beginning of the book relates my experiences of living in Paris, while establishing an English speaking theatre and presenting new plays, after working at the American Library there. The great restaurants and theatres were beyond the budget of our company of actors, at that time, but the joy of living in that city was compensation enough for many of us.

I have tried to weave a tapestry of sorts about the writers, actors, poets—both French and English speaking—who have become legends, whether it be 400 years ago or in the past century. It is not possible to include all of them. The other restaurants where all these thespians wined and dined are featured in a chapter of the book. They are all still in business, and some like the Grand Véfour have plaques on the tables in honour of the best of them.

INTRODUCTION

Paris means different things to everyone. Most Parisians love living there, obviously, otherwise they would relocate. For them, the city represents the vibrant, beating heart of their country, the nexus of government and business. For travellers it is always the first impression that you remember.

The city is one of the most visually beautiful in the world—from Notre Dame's glowering gargoyles to the Louvre's unforgettable painting of the Mona Lisa, to the glamorous can-can dancers at the Moulin Rouge, Paris offers the experience of a lifetime. Artists have written endlessly about the special quality of the light, the skies, the clouds and the inspiration they provoke, hence the oft-used "City of Lights" phrase.

Nowhere else does one find such a bustling center of paintings, sculpture, design, decoration, music, theatre, fashion—and literature. Indeed, writers feel the ambiance of the city—the cafés, the book-stalls, the history of the quartiers all stimulate the art of writing, whether it be a novel, a guide-book or a memoir. Gourmets and wine lovers are also caught up in the life of the city, searching out new pleasures and old by exploring and sometimes retracing their steps to a favourite bistro or restaurant. As has been written, meals can be memorable, but restaurants can leave behind lasting impressions.

On my last visit to Paris, though, I deliberately frequented untried restaurants rather than returning to favourite haunts, in search of new experiences. Restaurants with some kind of theatrical association were to me the most fascinating, whether it be because legendary actors of the theatre wined and dined there after their performances, or perhaps a playwright wrote or discussed an idea for a play there, or sat with his contemporaries before or after a play had been presented.

Arcade outside the Grand Vefour restaurant

The theatre within the Palais Royal, which was built in 1780 by Philippe, Duc d'Orléans, is a typical example. It is located right beside the legendary Grand Véfour restaurant, which occupies a class unto itself, well beyond its coveted three star-Michelin rating. Just around the corner sits the Comédie-Française—the national theatre of France—which houses a restaurant beside the stage door. The ghosts of Molière, Racine, Bernhardt, Voltaire must be walking about here all the time, the wind whistling through the arcades, spreading their spirits in one of the most beautiful squares in Paris. To think that one can pull up a chair at the same table Voltaire sat at for a memorable lunch, and peer through the same windows to admire the original Directoire interior…even the great Napoleon is rumoured to have dined here often with Josephine.

Upstairs window at Palais Royal—Colette's home was on the second
floor of the Palais Royal

The street that runs down the other side of these arcades is the Rue Beaujolais, and it was here where the famed French writer Colette lived at no. 9, in one of the apartments above the arcade where many other outstanding writers, artists and actors lived. The small shops in the arcade are still there, but not the same establishments. Chopin used to purchase his gloves at one of them, and no doubt he knew the place well.

Above the arches stands the old Hôtel Beaujolais, where Sylvia Beach, who founded the original Shakespeare & Company, first took up residence upon her arrival in Paris in 1917. Beach was actually en route to the southern part of France to work for the Red Cross, but looking out her Palais Royal window, she couldn't help but fall in love with the City of Light. During her stay, she met Adrienne Monnier, who ran a contemporary French literary bookshop. Beach was so inspired that she was soon back in Paris, opening her Anglo-American icon to literature, Shakespeare & Company, at 12 rue l'Odeon.

If visitors to Paris have a desire to capture the past glories of the legitimate theatre in Paris, where better than the Comédie-Française? Founded by a decree of Louis

XIV in 1680, it was the result of a merger of the only two Parisian acting troupes of the time, the troupe of the Hôtel Guénégaud and that of the Hôtel de Bourgogne. The repertoire back then consisted of the collection of theatrical works by Molière and Jean Racine, along with a few works by Pierre Corneille, Paul Scarron and Jean de Rotrou. Today, the Comédie-Française remains the only state theatre in France, and one of the few to have its own troupe of actors, with a repertoire of 3, 000 works and three separate theatres in the city (Salle Richelieu, next to the Palais Royal; Théâtre du Vieux-Colombier; and Studio-Théâtre).

The local "What's On", called "The Pariscope", lists all the theatres as well as the café-theatres which are located all over Paris. The night-clubs are usually in "caves", underground cellars on the left bank, where the air of passing time and times past fills the narrow streets, the antiques shops, the art galleries, restaurants and cafés.

It is difficult to compare the artistic areas of cities. For example, Covent Garden was the center of theatrical people for several centuries and still holds the aura of ghosts. The equivalent in Paris, I believe, is not the historical Marais district but the area around the Comédie-Française and the Palais Royal. The left bank was for the artists and writers but the proximity of the Tuileries and the gardens of the Palais Royal seem to capture the theatrical ambiance of Paris.

Comparing the location of theatres in the West End of London to the equivalent theatres in Paris is difficult too. The famous theatre at Le Chatelet, and the one on the Champs Elysees (on the right bank, on Avenue Marceau) could be offered, although the Theatre de la Ville de Paris on the left bank was also popular.

Although Edith Piaf and Colette were French, many legendary names associated with Paris were new arrivals. Singers tended to be more high profile than actors. Edith Piaf, Chevalier, Sacha Distel, Johnny Halliday, Sylvie Vartan, Juliette Greco, Claude, Yves Montand, Charles Aznavour, Jane Birkin, were all part of the theatrical scene. The French film stars Charles Boyer, Jean Gabin, Jean-Louis Trintignant, Jeanne Moreau—her debut in Jules and Jim brought her international fame—many became very popular in the States.

Among the other legendary artists who worked in Paris are Maria Callas, playwrights Sacha Guitry, Samuel Beckett, Jean Giraudoux. Jean Anouilh, Cocteau, Pagnol, and earlier Corneille, deMusset, Marivaux and dozens of others. Their rendezvous were all centered in the central part of Paris near the Opera, the Olympia, the Theatre des Champs Elysees.

Opera and ballet stars from across the world including Maria Callas, Joan Sutherland, Margot Fonteyn, and Rudolf Nureyev performed in the Opera Garnier, one of the most magnificent opera houses in the world. The Grand Salon in the Grand Hôtel, just opposite the opera house was often the venue for the receptions held before or after their performances. These salons can still be seen as well as the less grand and smaller rooms around these theatres.

The excitement of Broadway before curtain time is unique, but the same excited expectation can be found outside the Theatre de Chatelet, the Olympia, The Comédie-Française. After the performances, where do these audiences go? Some Americans go over to the Left Bank to La Coupole or Le Select to see where the lost generation of American writers of the 1920's congregated. They are now all so well known. Hemingway, Fitzgerald, and the Murphys are legendary, as are all the performers who worked then in Paris, including Josephine Baker and jazz artists from America who flocked to Paris, in part because of the relaxed attitude of the French towards the colour bar.

Today the younger generation have their new venues—which for some reason always seem to require loud music and strobe lighting even if the actors have just performed on stage. One wonders if they still want to dine at the older establishments that hold such memories and are slowly being modernised. This book endeavours to record and capture the romance of 20th century Paris, and the legendary theatrical personalities who worked there and made establishments famous by their patronage.

Comédie-Française, Salle Richelieu, exterior

1

ARRIVAL: FRENCH LESSONS

British thespians and food enthusiasts have always appreciated Paris, and many writers have worked and written about the city. But perhaps it is Americans who have written more than any other writers about their experiences in the last century, from Henry James to Ernest Hemingway, from Scott Fitzgerald to James Jones, all the way to present day writers such as David Sedaris, and Adam Gopnick. "When a James hero walks into a London drawing-room, our hearts sink for his embarrassments, but when he walks into a Paris hotel—no matter how poor his French may be, or how comic his prospects—our hearts lift a little at the promise of something that will be pleasurable in its unfolding. An American in Paris, is, as they say, a story in itself: one need merely posit it to have the idea of a narrative spring up, even if there is no narrative to tell."

The idea keeps its hold on us for a simple reason. For two centuries, Paris has been a fixture in the minds of many Americans as a symbol of happiness, of good things eaten and new clothes bought, and of a sentimental education achieved. Paris suggests the idea of happiness as surely as an arrival in New York suggests hope and Los Angeles, in literature at least, suggests hopelessness. It is the place to go to escape small-town, or even big-town American life and be happy. The Parisian idea is also an idea of happiness divorced, perhaps, from any idea of virtue, or even of freedom. The islands of license and permission that Americans find are surrounded by canals of order. But the idea of happiness sought and found in Paris is, more than merely an occasional episode in "travel writing," one of the haunting small themes of American literature. Paris is "the wonderful place, the only real capital of the world," wrote that entirely American writer William Dean Howells, and many of his brothers and sisters agree.

So it was on my arrival in Paris. The chestnut trees were in bloom all over the city and that feeling of happiness started all over again. It made me determined to stay in Paris to try to achieve something. It took planning but eventually it happened. We all know that throughout the centuries brilliant artists, writers, composers have lived here, and their work has become immortal. Here all achieved greatness, so why would anyone even begin to try to do any creative work while living in this city? It has all been done before. The cobblestones echo with the footsteps of a million artists, a million writers and composers who have trod in their footsteps trying to become immortal.

However the compensations are at least in keeping with the beauty of the city. The visual delights, including the architectural gems, and the artistic life are still accessible.

My story is very similar to countless others. I lived in Paris for four wonderful years and will never forget the experience. Returning there on subsequent visits, I found nothing much had changed. I tried to study French for several months in advance, but it is only when you live there that you really learn the language. The first few months trying to learn the language is by far the worst. David Sedaris has written a very humorous account of this nightmare which was very similar to mine, as I am sure it is the same French school of languages as we attended.

"If you have not meimslsxp or lgpdmurctrct by this time, then you should not be in this room. Has everyone apzkiubjxow? Everyone? Good, we shall begin." She spread out her lesson plan and sighed, saying, "All right then, who knows the alphabet?"

Then after that she asked us what were some of our favourite things. I used the wrong gender for a typewriter. The teacher's reaction led me to believe that these mistakes were capital crimes in France.

"Were you always this palicmkrexis? Even a fiuscrzsa ticiwelmun knows that a typewriter is feminine."

We soon learned to dodge chalk and protect our heads and stomachs whenever she approached us with a question. She hadn't yet punched anyone, but it seemed wise to protect ourselves against the inevitable.

Though we were forbidden to speak anything but French, the teacher would occasionally use us to practise any of her five fluent languages.

"I hate you," she said to me one afternoon. Her English was flawless. "I really hate you." Call me sensitive, but I couldn't help but take it personally.

Not only did my husband join the class, even though his French was pretty good, but we took our nine year old son Colman as well—so we all had the same home work to do. We were living in a very small, cheap hotel on the wrong end of the Rue de Rivoli, the Hôtel St. Marie, next door to the Samaritaine department store. In an effort to keep within a small budget, we would often decide to have some cold ham and cheese in our room for dinner. The hotel served only bright green soup and salad at night, which wasn't really sufficient. Bringing food into the hotel and up to your room was against the hotel rules, so we had great difficulty smuggling in our meal. We needed a baguette of course, which would be very noticeable carried through the lobby, so we used to put each half of a baguette up our sleeve jackets and walk stiff armed to the elevator, smiling at the girl as we passed the front desk.

Colman became great friends with the French couple who ran the hotel, and after we had been staying there for several months, they invited him to go with them on their annual vacation to the family farm down in the Jura region, in south west France. They had no children of their own and wanted to take him to spend a few weeks in August away from the heat and dust of Paris. I was very uncertain in handing over our son to relative strangers. He was gone a month, and I was anxious that he would be very lost in a family who only spoke French. However, when he returned he was like a little French boy, the total immersion had worked. So he had no further need to go to the Alliance Francaise with us.

Shortly afterwards we moved into an apartment and he started school at the local Ecole de Garcons (School for Boys). We lived nearby and he would come home and recite poetry in French, or speeches from a Molière play, as part of his homework. It was a true joy to listen to him as his accent was perfect. In fact, two years later when the school sent his class to the new English course, they were very surprised to learn that English was his native tongue.

One of the pleasures of living in Paris was to be out with him and hear him chatting along with his French friends or going to the theatre and having a translator beside you. He discovered the stamp market near the Rond Pointe and began his collection of tableau stamps. The sellers all knew him and he would discuss the various collections with them as his collection grew. A hobby which was a typical pastime for many schoolboys. Those albums are as good as photographs as momentos of our stay.

Then one day we discovered the Musee Grévin, the famous wax museum which still enchants children of all ages, named after Alfred Grévin, a cartoonist, sculptor, and theatrical costume designer. Grévin had been called upon by Arthur Meyer, a journalist and founder of the famous daily newspaper Le Gaulois, who at the end of the 19th Century had thought of creating three-dimensional likenesses of the front-page celebrities in his newspaper. This was at a time when the press did not use photography, and Meyer thought of establishing a place where people could at last "put a face" on the people in the news. The museum proved to be an immediate success upon opening its doors to the public on 5th June 1882, and continues to allow visitors to imagine they are up close with celebrities in the news—a visit to the Musee Grevin is a must if you are in Paris with children.

One afternoon in the Grévin Theatre—which is listed on the inventory of Historical Monuments—we watched a magician perform some incredible magic tricks. We went backstage to congratulate the performer, named Kassagi, who showed Colman a few extra tricks—from then on, we had a magician in the family. We found a shop on the left bank where professional magicians purchase their trick cards, boxes and vases. All pocket money went from buying stamps to buying magic props. Trick razor blades you can swallow, sharp cutters which can cut off a finger if you don't know the trick—so we had now had a son whose only ambition was to become a magician and work at the Musee Grevin. The die was cast.

As my son began discovering these intriguing passions, so too would I explore the many dimensions of this grand city and the historical traditions it carries with it—beginning with the discovery of the American library—a visit that would prove to open a series of doors into a world of literature, theatre and history that I could never have imagined.

2

THE AMERICAN LIBRARY IN PARIS

Ever since I had arrived in Paris all I knew was that I wanted to stay, to live, to work in that wonderful city. To experience the changing of the seasons, their celebrations on Bastille Day, their customs and food planned for Christmas and other feast days, to discover the charm of little known museums, historic places and above all the theatre and restaurants. But my French was not good, and I needed practice, so where on earth would I find a job?

My lucky break came one morning while I was walking around the Champ-de-Mars, the vast public stretch of parkland in the 7th arrondissement between the Eiffel Tower to the northwest and the École Militaire (Military School) to the southeast, one of the most charming residential areas in Paris. Translated as "Field of Mars", the area was named after Mars, the Roman god of war, and its initial purpose was to serve as a training ground for military manoeuvres. Today, lakes, ornamental ponds, winding walks and grottoes adorn the area, which is home to many birds and one of the rare places in Paris where the song of the tawny owl can be heard at night.

I decided to venture onto a side street, chancing upon a building called the American Library. My curiousity aroused, I found the door open and walked right in. I found it a fascinating place, and after listening to various conversations among the staff at the front desk, I soon learned they were shorthanded, it seemed, so I started talking with them and ended up asking for a job. This seemed to be the perfect place—the timing was right, and I ended up working there for two years. Every day I walked to work from the little hotel we were staying at, and the beauty of the Paris knocked me out. Each morning I would walk across the bridge beside the Louvre, along the quais, and passed the bridges, the open markets, the fabulous buildings, the fruit shops and the cafés.

The job at the Library proved fascinating. I immediately met all the subscribers, all the newcomers at the Front Desk. Most Americans living in Paris came in to borrow books or read magazines and newspapers from the States. If we were not busy I would talk with them, ask why they were here, how long they had been here and found out about their work and lives in France. There was a two-hour lunch break and a half-day off. It was heaven to go back into the stacks and delve among books that made your mouth water. Signed editions of Gertrude Stein and Hemingway etc. plus all the French writers, many translated into English.

After a few months of this, an idea began to form in my mind as to how I could combine living in Paris, working in the theatre and keep acting as well. There were many French students coming into the Library to read American and English playwrights. They waited, sometimes for weeks, on a request list for the one-act plays of Pinter, Albee, Tennessee Williams and any new plays that had been written. There was no possibility of these students seeing these plays on stage in English. They had to go home and try to sit and read them with the aid of an English or American dictionary.

I thought to myself, why not present these plays to them in English? These plays were set for their University exams—they had papers to write on them. Wouldn't it be a lot easier for them if they could actually see the play?

There were other reasons too—it would give French students the opportunity of seeing well-known plays in English, it would provide entertainment for English-speaking tourists and residents who didn't know enough French to go to a French play, and also function as a showcase for new plays and performers from the United States and England. It would fulfill a need, as far as the students were concerned and also give new playwrights who were writing in Paris a chance to present their plays too.

Sounded great. Paris. My own theatre. The toast of the Ritz. Discovering new playwrights hidden in garrets in Paris, saving them from suicide. Seriously though, I thought there might be people working in Paris who would be interested. I used to pass Sylvia Beach's old shop every week and remember James Joyce, Samuel Beckett and all the other writers who had a tough time of it in

Paris. Maybe there were a few now, in our generation, writing and not hearing from New York for months on end.

It was then that I met Roland and Jennie. They were there for the same reason that I was, to experience the city, to learn French and to create and express something of themselves in some way—*any way*—if they could just get it out from being all bottled up inside. They had brought their three-year-old with them from Ohio, so they were more restricted in their activities than I was. Nevertheless they had managed to find a place to live, and the fact that they had both started to write impressed me immensely. Both of them had worked in the theatre back in the States, and they were enthusiastic about my idea of forming a theatre company in Paris. Roland became our first Director.

So now I had found a structured life at last. I found an apartment. I could speak French well enough to get along at dinner parties—the ultimate test I think—and I had found something I really wanted to do and could see more point to doing it than anything else at that time. There is a time and place for everything and this was it, as far as I was concerned.

3

OPENING OUR OWN THEATRE

We started advertising for authors and scripts. From ads placed in the Paris papers we received replies from all over France. It seemed as if there were American writers hidden away all over the country—from the Loire, the Indre, the Basque country down to, or rather up to, Normandy.

Some of the plays were in verse, some were all four-letter words, some were pages of revue skits, some were long one-act monologues from freaky people. We read them all and were amazed that these people had actually found places to live in the French countryside and that they had organized themselves to such a degree, had the tenacity and money to stick it out *then* sit down and write. It was difficult enough to do it in Paris, but deep in the country somewhere, where the heating probably never worked, where the isolation, the plumbing, the physical discomforts must have been even worse to put up with than in Paris.

Auditions were held, and we chose a company of actresses and actors, some of whom were from the States, others from England and Canada. Rehearsals started on a verse play by a chap from Sussex who was now living in Normandy. He wrote a cooking column for "Vogue" magazine every so often (so we knew what *he* did for fulfilment if his writing wasn't going very well).

That's one great advantage of living in France—when things get really rough or really rotten, you can eat. And eat the most heavenly food you can imagine. There is always that perfect piece of Brie and fresh bread, with a carafe of wine or some glorious pastry, or delicious pate, waiting at practically every corner in every village or at your local market.

It seems to make it all worthwhile. The frustrations, the rages, the confusion of just-where-do-think-you-are-going-with-your-life, can be countered by the complete sensual enjoyment of the country in the Spring and Summer and sometimes Autumn, after a delicate lunch in the country—three or four courses perhaps, tiny courses of perfect food with a good wine. These are the saving graces that can carry one through the toughest of times.

Anyway, to get back to Paris again. We started rehearsing the play. The actors were good. We were all working for practically no money at all but we all felt we were doing something *worthwhile*. The rehearsals were very long, held in cold rehearsal halls—we worked hard and often in places where we were freezing to death.

The French staff at the various rehearsal rooms thought we were stark crazy, and said so. An English-language theatre in Paris? Who would go? We were presenting plays that had never been done before, anywhere, and in English. Perhaps when we did Tennessee Williams or Albee or Pinter, someone might come. Maybe those enthusiastic students from the Sorbonne who could digest anything, but always seemed to have an intense fascination with the American Red Indian. I can't tell you how many French students I met in the Library who would read anything they could get their hands on about the "Peaux Rouges". We met one guy who was leaving his wife, child and a newborn baby to go off to some Mid-Western university to take a course about the Red Indian.

There was no time left to sit around and discuss the policy of the theatre, the use of drama, the "meaning of theatre", we had to get on with it. I met at least two people who had tried running a theatre there before, and they said we were mad and that we would never survive, no one would come, and that if we had any success—financial success, that is—we would be closed down by the French authorities on some cute pretext, such as that we might be putting other actors out of work—French actors.

Next, the search for a theatre began. We wanted a small place with an intimate atmosphere. I criss-crossed Paris day after day looking in all kinds of places. Some were absolute gems—an old theatre in a private "hotel" or an ornately carved assembly hall with minstrel gallery still intact. But they were always too big, or too small, or the rent was too high.

It took three weeks before I found "Le Poteau" on the Right Bank. Le Poteau means "the post" in English and we soon found out why. There was a post just right of centre stage, on stage, which was holding up the ceiling. But oddly enough it didn't look too bad.

I knew as soon as I walked in the door that I had found our place.

The theatre itself was tiny with banquettes around the walls and a bar at the back—the "ambience" was terrific. As for the post on stage, well, it just made the stage directions all the more challenging. The actors had to be on their toes if they didn't want to crash into it every so often—and bring the house down in more ways than one.

We moved in with our props, wardrobe and gear and started final rehearsals for the first night, a first night that seemed headed for disaster. The leading lady had caught the flu and had lost her voice, the leading man refused to follow the stage director's directions and had resigned a week before the opening night. He said his contract wasn't binding (it wasn't, in France)—so we were left with their two understudies. For our opening night!

One understudy was a theatre student, not really experienced enough to play a lead, and the other male understudy was a part-time ballet dancer, who was not really suitable for the heavy male lead required in the play.

To say that I didn't sleep very well that week would be a ridiculous understatement. I wanted to phone all my friends and beg them not to come on the opening night. The publicity was already out. Ads in the "Pariscope" and the Paris "What's On" etc. Everything was just too late to stop or to do anything about.

Only one week earlier I had received the theatre posters and was terribly impressed with them. I suppose only someone with an ego as large as mine would appreciate what it is like driving around Paris and sticking up posters of "our theatre"—I posted a lot of them myself for the pure pleasure. It felt great sticking on one at "Le Dome", "Aux Deux Magots", "La Rotonde"—all the cafés where Hemingway and Fitzgerald and the "lost generation" hung out. It didn't matter to me really that I was about thirty years too late to impress them or entice them to my theatre.

It was a mad afternoon going around the Left Bank dropping off these purple posters, then driving home again along the Boulevard St. Germain and seeing them all staring out at me. But that was last week. This week was different.

I felt like disappearing and letting the stage-manager take over till after the first night. But as founder and producer what could I do?

The night before the opening night my next-door neighbour in my apartment building decided to practise his violin (he was a violinist with the Paris Symphony Orchestra), together with the violin and the tension of opening night, my sleep was racked with more than the usual nightmares that most performers go through before an opening night—with the exception that I wasn't performing—just sitting in a (perhaps) empty theatre—me, and the drama critic from the International Herald Tribune in Paris, both of us watching a disaster take place up there on the stage.

But as we all know, some of our worst fears never come true—just some, mind you, and this one didn't.

The opening night was a success, and it was some kind of miracle to see people coming in the door and not turning away. It *was* a miracle! People kept coming in—we had no place to seat all of them. There was standing room only for our first night. Tom Quinn Curtis from the Herald Tribune came along and was kind enough to give us a good review and say nice things about us.

We had begun.

Our second production was a crazy comedy by the English playwright N. F. Simpson "A Resounding Tinkle". This play is filled with funny non-sequiturs and silly things about unusual people. It was a risk to do it because we didn't know whether our French audience would understand any of it. But we wanted to do it and hoped that at least the French students would catch some of the funny lines. Lines like:

BRO: "Oh hullo, Uncle Ted, where did you park your motorcycle?"

UNCLE TED: "On the spare lot, behind Rachmaninoff's Second Piano Concerto."

It was a bit difficult for an English-born playgoer to follow, let alone a Frenchman.

One evening we had a Frenchman sitting, alone, in the third row listening intently to everything that was said—he seemed to understand English very well—suddenly he went into absolute hysterics, doubling over and then falling backwards in his seat. This happened approximately every five minutes or so, especially when any actor made his entrance. I couldn't figure out if he really *could* understand all the dialogue—as I said, it was pretty funny—or whether he was laughing hysterically at the acting, the costumes or what. I only knew that he was a great lift to the audience and loved by the cast.

We kept seeing new people and talking with writers. Every day I met people who were either screaming with rage over life in Paris, or in fits of depression, or in raptures of delight, or bored out of their minds, or inspired and stimulated beyond their wildest dreams. It happens this way, you can experience all these things within the course of, say, one week. Especially if you are trying to write, or paint or follow some creative endeavour. The actual "feeling" and nervous energy, if you can call it that, is what Paris is all about, as far as I'm concerned.

The theatre was a great release, we rehearsed, we talked, we sat in cafés after work, in marvellous art deco-cafés with great faces of interesting characters surrounding us—stimulus for playwrights searching for characters—and all of us in the group felt we were achieving something, though we weren't sure what. We weren't writing the plays ourselves admittedly, but we were in contact with the people who were, and with people who had the same nervous energy that we had.

Is it just student "neurosis", this nervous energy to create? Sometimes I think it is, but then, how come we still have middle-aged writers? They must have screaming fits of rage, despair, hope, depression, suffering, just as young people have. I would like to hear from writers who don't suffer any more.

Sometimes after the performance at the theatre I would stay behind in the bar and talk to any patrons who had stayed on to have an after-play drink. I talked to a lot of tourists too—couples from the Mid-West or Canada or the English provinces, people who didn't understand French well enough to go to a French theatre, or didn't want to go to another strip-show or a movie with sub-titles, and so would come to us. I used to talk to the women if they stayed—mostly housewives on a one-week holiday in Paris. Perhaps a school-teacher or nurse. I'd search their faces for signs of what kind of lives they lived, it fascinated me.

Having our own theatre in Paris we were on our way. We were reading scripts from writers living all over Europe. The mail was a delight. That was one of the great pleasures about the whole venture. Now at last, after years of just receiving bills, handouts, local folders, church newsletters, auction sale announcements, more bills, traffic tickets, over-due notices, I was receiving fascinating letters, plays, resumes, life-stories of people whom I could identify with, ideas, scripts for revues—all of which was more broadening than any cocktail party introductions or dinner party friends, which I had a steady diet of for years.

There were some days when I felt we were achieving a great deal, and other days when it seemed that we were all just working very hard, being very idealistic and not achieving very much at all.

We still met in cafés after the show and discussed our aims and future plans—hour after hour. I felt the aim of the theatre was to promote new ideas and most of all to promote "thought". I didn't want to present any plays which didn't do that. To make people stop and think about our play was what mattered to me the most.

But some of those early days were hell. First of all, there were the terrific mood swings of everybody concerned. It is not unusual, I'm sure, in any troupe who are working together, but it seemed harder starting off a new venture and a new company, then trying hard to be as idealistic as possible. My own mood swings were very hard to cope with, especially as I was living on my own with no one to discuss the finer details with, the decisions, the general over-all plans that had to be made. The company was pulling its weight, working hard, but I was the one who had to make the decisions.

The company would change about and casts would change too. We couldn't pay very much money to any of our actors so they usually had to move on—back to the States or on to England.

We had a nucleus of about ten people who stayed on, however, and most of them had part-time jobs elsewhere in the daytime, teaching English part-time or working in offices, or studying at the University with a grant from home. Fortunately all of them had worked professionally in the theatre, so we had a well-trained group who were, in general, as enthusiastic as I was.

The cold weather seemed to keep people away from the theatre. Our theatre, anyway. We worried about insufficient heat in the theatre, and whether people would return if they thought much about how cold they were; we prayed for an early Spring.

The theatre was full of people with colds, coughs, sinus trouble. My God! I was beginning to feel the whole of Paris was full of people with colds, sniffers, coughers, spitters and more and more coughers. One night standing behind the bar, I just nearly went out of my mind listening to them and could easily have wrung the necks of everybody sitting in the audience. Shut up! For Christ's sake! Or Get Out. I *had* to get out. I walked across the street to the corner bistro and ordered a brandy at the zinc counter—even the barman coughed. When would Spring come? This was getting impossible. We couldn't go on much longer this way. All of us were getting very frayed and most of the troupe had to go home to freezing rooms after walking along freezing streets after being in a freezing theatre all night.

Needless to say the theatre owner would do nothing about improving the heat—it was "on" after all, what more could he do? He would say this every week with a typical shrug of the shoulders and the out-stretched palms.

We decided to close for a week and those of us who could get out of Paris and get down south for a while started to make plans.

It was on one of my "up" days or rather "up" evenings when I arrived at the train station to catch the train to Cannes, otherwise the whole thing would have been a disaster.
I had thought of flying down, but to miss all that glorious French country between the Loire Valley and the south coast seemed sinful. So I thought I'd try seeing some of it just once, then after that one could fly, guiltlessly over it forever after.

You are asked when you buy your ticket if you want to go first or second class, and do you want a couchette? I said "second class" and "yes". I did want a couchette. (A small bed, usually bunk type, three each side of the cabin, one of top of the other). Better than sitting up all night as the train journey took twelve hours, starting at 6 pm.

I found the platform and the train, the guard showed me onto the carriage and then to my compartment. He took me straight to the cubicle with the six couchettes, pointed to the middle one, said "Voila" and then disappeared.

Maybe we all have countries waiting for us which will show us what we really should be doing. What you are doing now, might only be a shadow of what you really could be doing in—well, say Australia or Spain or wherever.

I certainly wouldn't have been running a theatre back home, for example, the idea never occurred to me.

Perhaps that is one of the reasons why France means so much to so many people. It provokes so much emotion, either rage or pleasure, that one is constantly seeking expression and release (the stimulus and frustrations of one's own goals) seeing new horizons, new work, and generally growing by having to pull oneself up the the hair roots, or whatever the expression is.

Back in Paris again and back to work. The weather was warm, the company rested. Enthusiasm had returned and we once again felt that what we were doing was still as worthwhile and as fresh as when we first thought of the idea.

We were rehearsing a new play by a playwright from Tennessee and we were sure it would be our best production to date. It was a comedy and the parts were well written. The critic from the Tribune thought so too, and we had a good run and good audiences for the play. If this sounds as if things were running smoothly and we were all sitting around congratulating ourselves, then I give a false impression. I don't think anything, or anybody in any relationship can run "smoothly" in Paris for more than, say, two days at a time.

It's just something about the city that does it.

4

LIVING IN PARIS

During these years I followed the theatre in Paris as well as my knowledge of French would allow. In the first year I would take an English or dual script of the play with me to the Comédie-Française. I discovered the seats where the bright overhead safety lights were left on. They were like EXIT signs but without lettering. However there was enough light to be able to read the English script at the same time as watching the play on stage. Also, listening to the play on tape in French at home and following it in English was very helpful.

If other theatres had plays I wanted to see, I would try to read the play first even in French, as then I could at least understand most of the action. Modern plays were more difficult because the language contained more argot (slang) and colloquial idioms, for instance "I've got other cats to whip."

Often there were interesting lectures on Sunday nights at the Palais Royal which were difficult to follow at times, or dramatisations of the life of Oscar Wilde or Alfred de Musset or George Sand, usually made up of dramatic scenes with music when appropriate. They were elegant soirées which were cleverly devised and produced. How fascinating to sit in one of the most beautiful theatres in France watching French actors recount the life of a celebrated artist or writer.

Some days the fatigue and anxiety of a long week spent coping with the language, the housekeeping, the travelling, would be relieved by going to one of the American bars in town and having a few strong gin-and-tonics. It is a curious thing however, that the well-known cocktail bars of the 20's, the Ritz, the Bristol, the Hôtel Continental, were usually deserted at 6 pm. We could never figure it out whether we were too early or too late.

Theatre actors are held in high regard and were more respected than cinema stars. Jean Piat—the French equivalent of perhaps Nigel Patrick, Simon Williams, Alan Alda or Simon Callow—was not only celebrated for his work as a classical actor, but also in Boulevard theatre, popular, modern theatre. Most of his contemporaries worked more in the theatre than in films.

Occasionally visiting companies provided some English speaking theatre. The Abbey Theatre from Dublin played for a short season in "She Stoops to Conquer" and the National Theatre came as well. The other source of enjoyment was following the up-coming programs at the Olympia. Although music-hall, it has the same excitement as New York's Radio City Music-Hall or the Palladium in London. French stars have all appeared there, including Edith Piaf, Charles Aznavour, Yves Montand, Sacha Distel and visiting stars such as Liza Minelli, Jerry Lewis (he was adored in Paris even though his act included his speaking an imitation of nonsensical French but with the right gestures). Most Parisians regard the Olympia as the home for all the superstars.

If you enjoyed meeting these kinds of celebrities, all you had to do was to visit the little bar which was just around the corner from the stage door. I discovered it when I went to interview Sacha Distel for a magazine article. But maybe that secret has already been discovered.

Paris is not an easy city to live in. It is more difficult than New York or London. Not only the language but the day-to-day routines are so different. In New York there are many stores and cafés open 24 hours, Duane Reade being one of them. But in Paris, if you want to go grocery shopping after lunch, forget it. Everything is closed till late afternoon, except the supermarkets which are hell on earth compared to those in the U. S. or U. K. The transportation is more complicated and tiring, long passageways between subway stations and the air is much dirtier than in other cities. People are less polite, especially shop-keepers. I used to think that their bad tempers were because of the cheap red wine they drank at lunch and then tried to sleep off without success.

When the weather turns cold it is far more bitterly cold than anything I've ever known elsewhere. The damp iciness is unforgettable, it lingers inside stairwells and passageways that never seem to become warm even in summer. It is a particular cold that is extremely depressing, as it comes with a cold grey mist and bleak skies. I remember visiting the Père Lachaise cemetery on such a day, death seemed to be very gruesome and near, with the chilling silent tombs on the other side of my path. Chilled to the bone was an apt expression.

But for whatever misgivings I might have had about the climate, the thrill of being in the middle of one of the greatest cities in Europe, and exploring so much historical—and culinary—culture more than made up for the physical discomforts. This exploration would unfold as I discovered more of Paris' famous theatrical institutions, which deserve a chapter in their own right.

5

THE THEATRES OF PARIS

There are three basic kinds of theatres in Paris. The first is the official state theatre, the Comédie-Française, which is under the control of the Ministry of Fine Arts and subsidised by the French Government. The plays of Corneille, Racine and Molière are the fundamental repertoire, with the addition of a few 18th and 19th century plays by such authors as Marivaux, Beaumarchais, and Musset.

A second state theatre, the Théâtre National Populaire, also subsidized but with a smaller budget, is intended to bring theatre to a more popular and larger audience, with a more modest repertoire and more foreign plays. The second kind of theatre is privately owned, deriving its character from notable directors, who become stars in their own right, as do popular actors such as Edwige Feuillere and Maria Casares—predominantly women, a tradition that did not end with Sarah Bernhardt.

The third type of theatre is the avant-garde, powered by such playwrights as Beckett, Adamov, Ghelderode, Ionesco, Pichette and Schehade, and preceded by Sartre, Anouilh in the 1940s, and earlier by Cocteau, Montherlant, Giraudoux, etc. In the avant-garde theatre, character and plot are largely subordinated to ideas, particularly of a a religious, philosophical and political kind.

It is interesting to note that there are three kinds of eating establishments in Paris as well: first are the elegant restaurants which could be compared with the elegance of the classical theatre such as the Comédie-Française; then there are the bistros and brasseries, which are akin to the commercial or boulevard theatres; and lastly the café-theatres, often actually found in basements of cafes and bars that are the breeding ground for new plays, revues and discovering new actors.

The biggest theatre in all of Europe remains the Théâtre National de Chaillot, one of only five National Theatres in France—not to be confused with the Comédie-Française. Launched by the famous French actor Firmin Gémier on November 11, 1920, at the Palais de Chaillot, on the site of the old Trocadero, as the Théâtre National Populaire, the venue was inspired by the dramatic and theoretical works of Romain Rolland as well as Maurice Pottecher. Renamed the Théâtre du Palais de Chaillot in 1938 under director Paul Abram, it became a central focus of Parisian cultural life following the World War Two, under the leadership of Jean Vilar, and with actors like Gérard Philippe and Maria Casares.

The theatre's 1200 seats outstrips the 700 of Drury Lane, the 600 of the Palladium; it is twice the size of the Old Vic, and three times as big as the Haymarket. Its stage is huge enough to accommodate five hundred chorus-girls—not even the Radio City Music Hall in New York is as large!

The Marigny Theatre, by the side of the open-air stamp market in the Champs Elysées, is another historic venue, which holds almost exactly the same seats as the Piccadilly Theatre in London. The theatre played host to the debut on May 7th, 1921, of the French adaptation (by Henri Berté) of Franz Schubert's operetta Das Dreimäderlhaus, dubbed Chanson d'amour (Song of Love), and subtitled La maison des trois jeunes filles (The House of the Three Young Girls).

The Marigny was later where the celebrated Jean-Louis Barrault/Madeleine Renaud company would give many dazzling performances, with musical director Pierre Boulez at the helm. (They took over the theatre in 1946 and went to London in 1951 where they produced a season of plays). Later the theatre would feature "The Beautiful Indifferent One," a one-act play by Jean Cocteau which Edith Piaf performed in 1953, with sets designed by Lila de Nobili and choreography by Raymond Rouleau, with Jacques Pills, her husband, as her partner.

The normal London or New York theatre conforms to the same national pattern. It is an average-sized place, seating about a thousand people or a couple of hundred more. But generally speaking, apart from a few monster-size theatres, the Parisian theatres are smaller, with an astonishing sixteen as small as—or smaller than—the Fortune in London or the Helen Hayes in New York. As a result, the tiny confines of these theatres encourage the writing of light and frothy little farces and comedies, without enough substance to fill a big playhouse. One does not ask for elaborate plays in a theatre hardly larger than a drawing-room.

It has been said that English audiences remember what they see, French audiences what they hear. Indeed, the French theatre is one in which the presiding genius is the author.

The evolution of French theatrical form has no doubt been influenced by the small size of most Parisian theatres, which lift a great strain from the actors' voices. However quietly or casually they speak, their words can be heard in every part of the house. They can also be clearly seen by the audience, nor merely in bulk but in detail.

French actors who succeeded in exploiting this intimate environment to positive effect included Henry Guisol, the husband in "Le Complexe de Philemon" who so disturbs the psychiatrist by being obstinately faithful to his wife, or Robert Vattier, the husband in Andre Roussin's "Nina", who is overwhelmed with naive admiration for the multiple conquests of his wife's lover. These actors indulged in a richness of facial play what would go for nothing in most London theatres—for the excellent reason that it would be invisible at the back of the stalls and dress-circle, and in the upper circle and gallery.

But at the Monceau, the Michel, or the Wagram, a wink is as easily seen as an epileptic fit at the Prince's or Winter Garden. Stendhal, writing of Julien Sorel's embarrassed silence in the presence of women, says in compensation that his eyes flashed "like a good actor's." This is not an English novelist's metaphor—one could go to theatres every week for half a century in either London or the British provinces, and still not be able to tell whether actors' eyes flash or not.

This interesting contrast is only one of many that has given France it's own unique set of theatrical traditions over the last 400 years, ever since the days of Molière—whose life and times begin our colourful journey into the rich history of French theatre.

6

MOLIÈRE—FRANCE'S GREATEST PLAYWRIGHT

Comédie-Française, Salle de la Comédie-Française, Galerie des bustes—Busts of French playwrights

The life of French theatre writer, director and actor, Molière—generally considered France's greatest writer of comedies, and rated by many critics as the foremost of all French writers—is one also filled with constant struggle, hard work, domestic turmoil, ending in death and burial in obscurity and practically shame. Although he enjoyed a good deal of popularity and success, he nevertheless endured attacks and persecution for his work satirizing the hypocrisy and pretentions of middle and upper class French society. He left behind him an impressive body of work which not only changed the face of French classical comedy, but has gone on to influence the work of other dramatists the world over.

Molière was born in Paris, in a house thought to be on the Rue St Honore, on January 15, 1622, as Jean-Baptiste Poquelin. He was the son of Marie Cressé and Jean Poquelin, a well-to-do upholsterer and furniture merchant, the descendant of a long line of Beauvais tradesmen. His father had obtained the privilege of supplying the royal court, one of eight such "valets de chambre tapissiers" who tended the king's furniture and upholstery. As a result, the young Poquelin had the benefit of every advantage a boy could wish for, including an excellent education at one of the finest schools in Paris at the time, the College de Clermont, a prestigious Jesuit school where he had a strict upbringing and studied Latin and Greek. It was at Clermont that Poquelin first would have become acquainted with Latin, Spanish, and Italian comedies, as well as ballets, of which he later became a distinguished master. He remained at the college until he was sixteen before moving to Orléans to study law, and was said to have been awarded a law degree in 1642.

Despite all the privileges bestowed on him, he took great pleasure in poking fun at the aristocracy, creating quite a stir by imitating the priest of his mother, a deeply religious woman, who died in 1632 when he was only ten years old. Although his father remarried the following year, his second wife also passed away within less than three years, leaving Jean-Baptiste alone with his father, who would have likely apprenticed him in the business of upholstering, at his shops in the covered Halle de la Foire, and Saint Germain des Prés. As Poquelin turned 18, he inherited the the title of Tapissier du Roi, and the associated office of valet de chambre, an appointment that saw him in frequent contact with the king, and he likely accompanied Louis XIII to Provence in 1642 as his valet tapissier.

But just around the corner from his father's shop, a couple of theatrical sites were to have a big impact on the young Poquelin: the Hôtel de Bourgogne—where he went with his grandfather to watch the King's Players perform traditional romantic tragedies and broad farces—and the Pont-Neuf, where he spent many an afternoon marvelling at comedians performing plays and farces in the street in an effort to foist sell various medicines on the audience. These early exposures to the performing arts led to his decision in 1643, at the age of twenty-one, to turn away from both the legal profession and his father's business, giving up his claim to succeed his father as valet de chambre du roi, and instead dedicating his life to the theatre.

Armed with this passion for the theatre—coupled with his association with the head of a Parisian troupe of Italian comedians—the young Poquelin set his sights on becoming an actor in 1643, joining the company of a beautiful red-headed actress by the name of Madeleine Béjart, who subsequently became his mistress for many years. Along with Joseph and Genevieve Bejard, and about a dozen other young well-to-do hopefuls, they set upon reconverting an old tennis court into a stage for dramatic performances, marking the birth of the financially shaky dramatic troupe called The Illustrious Theatre, or "Illustre-Theatre"—illustre a then-slang expression liberally employed by writers at the time.

It was around this period that he adopted his stage name of Molière from a popular novelist—likely in an effort to save his father from the embarrassment of having an actor in the family. The theatre saw modest success, acquiring the patronage of Philippe d'Orléans, and appearing in three different theatres in various parts of Paris. But despite its youthful enthusiasm, few of the players had much experience and when they began to charge admission, the results proved disastrous. Molière, who had become head of the troupe, went bankrupt, was arrested by the tradesman who supplied candles, and actually spent time in the Grand Chatelet prison for debt. His father came to the rescue, getting him released, after which the young Molière left Paris with Madeleine, gathering together a group of actors for a tour of the French provinces, chiefly in the south—a tour which lasted about ten years.

It was in the spring of 1658 that Molière first learned that the Duke of Anjou, brother of the young King Louis XIV, was expressing interest in sponsoring a dramatic company to bear his name. The budding playwright and actor immediately worked to garner an introduction to the Royal Court, leading to his debut performance before Louis XIV and his courtiers in the Guard Room of the old Louvre Palace on the evening of October 24, 1658. Molière was subsequently awarded the title of Troupe de Monsieur, and allowed to share a Parisian theatre with a popular Italian troupe of actors, the Hôtel du Petit Bourbon, one of the three most important theatres in Paris, which Molière became sole lessee of the following year. The Hôtel first saw the production, on November 18, 1659, of "Les Précieuses Ridicules" (or The Pretentious Ladies, also known as The High-Brow Ladies), a farce satirizing certain mannerisms and affected speech then common in France, particularly among the salons and the literary ladies whose chief aim in life was to promote culture.

The play was a hit, and proved to be the turning point in Molière's career, not only as a theatre director, but also catapulting him into current literary debate. He was able to double the price of admission, even garnering an invitation to give a special performance for the King—who was so delighted that he endowed Molière with a large monetary gift. But the playwright did not enjoy the same respect among some of the King's inner circle—including Madame de Rambouillet, who had performances of the play suspended for fourteen days and eventually closed the Petit Bourbon completely, in an effort to expel Molière from the capital. But the King stepped in and appointed Molière and his colleagues official providers of entertainment, granting them use of the Théâtre du Palais Royal, where he would continue to perform for the rest of his life.

In the following 24 years, Molière progressed from skillfully adapting Italian-based sketches and a producer of extravaganzas to a gifted playwright of tragedies with lasting impact. He gradually perfected his style, as both dramatist and chief actor, continuing to present works full of intrigue and adventure more in keeping with the older school. With his own work, however, he trail-blazed a new genre, setting his sights not only on the sentimental blue-stockings and the lacklustre patrons of the French salons, but also priests, doctors, nobles, and even actors—no one was immune from his comic wit.

He is regarded by many as the father of French high comedy, exposing the hypocrisies and follies of his society through satire, and establishing the groundwork for future French comedy writing, ranking alongside such greats as Plautus and George Bernard Shaw. The great variety in his work can be attributed to his being at once actor, director, stage manager, and writer. He penned twelve of the most enduring and penetratingly sarcastic comedies ever, both in prose and regular dramatic verse, along with six shorter farces and comedies. His repertoire also extended to pastorals and comedy-ballets, produced on short notice for the entertainment of the court, and which often relied on a impressive collection of staging equipment that worked to execute swift and spectacular changes of scenes.

During this intensive, demanding career, Molière suffered repeatedly from pulmonary complaints, and in the late 1660s, he developed a lung ailment to which he finally succumbed to during a performance in the title role of "Le malade imaginaire" (The Hypochondriac or Imaginary Invalid, 1673)—a play partly based on his own sad life and illness, and featuring the character Argan, a hypochondriac afraid of death and of doctors.

During the fourth performance of the play, on February 17, 1673, Molière suffered a hemorrhage and collapsed on stage. He had reportedly insisted on continuing with the performance—in spite of the advice of his wife and friends—saying, "There are fifty poor workers who have only their daily wage to live on. What will become of them if the performance does not take place?" He was taken to his home on the Rue Richelieu, where he died at ten o'clock at the same night—without sacraments because two priests refused to visit him (actors had no social standing and had been excommunicated by the church) and the third arrived too late. Since no priest was present at his bedside, he was hence refused sanctified burial, and his wife Armande had to beg Louis XIV to intercede on her behalf with the Archbishop of Paris so that Molière could be properly buried, a right most actors forfeited by their choice of profession. Four days later, the King interceded and Molière was finally buried in the Cemetery Saint Joseph under the cover of darkness.

As with so many details of his life, accounts of his funeral consist of legend mixed with fact; most describe of a secret burial, while others refer to more normal last rites, in light of the Molière's solid middle-class standing as holder of the family's upholstery privilege. Seven years later the king merged Molière's troupe with one of its competitors to become the founding nucleus of today's Comédie-Française, the French national theatre, which has been known as the House of Molière ever since. During the following century his bust was placed in the Academy, and a monument erected over his grave. In 1792 his remains were brought to the museum of French monuments and in 1817 transferred to Le Père Lachaise Cemetery, Paris, close to La Fontaine.

7

GEORGE SAND—GREATEST WOMAN PLAYWRIGHT

"The greatest thing in life is to love...and to be loved"

—George Sand.

George Sand (Aurore Dudevant), one of the most celebrated women writers in history, was also probably the most energetic and passionate people of her own time. Descended from the Marchal de Saxe, she was also related through him to King Casimir of Poland. After a fairly conventional education she married a member of the local nobility, Baron Dudevant, by whom she had a daughter Solange. George and her husband were not compatible in any way and separated after a few years of marriage.

In order to support herself and her daughter, she had to find some form of employment, and realistically the only one open to her was as a writer. Her first works were stories of rural life, represented as romantic, its inhabitants idealised, as in her best known novel of that period "La Petite Fadette". Her later novels became progressively more realistic and achieved enormous popularity not merely in France, but also throughout Europe, including Russia.

Politics was a matter of serious interest to her; she wrote extensively on political subjects from a populist, anti-authoritarian point of view. Not only did she write over 50 novels, but she once had four of her plays running simultaneously in Paris. Only the British writer Somerset Maugham could match that.

She was most famous for her novels and political life as well as for being the mistress of Chopin. They lived together in her Paris apartment and later at Nohant, her country estate below the Loire Valley in central France.

Her biographers all write of her fame and her celebrated life. She wrote through the night when she had the undisturbed time to work; the day-time hours were for her children and Chopin. She dressed in men's clothing when she first went to Paris, to enable her to disguise her gender and therefore be taken as seriously as a man—in her writing and her socializing, in the theatre pits where the cheaper seats were where only men were allowed.

In the chateau at Nohant, she had a tiny theatre built on the ground floor. It was here that she would rehearse and try out her new plays. She also wrote short scenes for her dinner companions or house guests. Chopin often took part either acting or playing music for the scene changes. This small theatre can still be seen today, with the stage still set with furnishings for a scene from one of her plays.

Chopin went to Majorca with her to try to recover from tuberculosis but the stay only worsened his condition because of bad weather. She took him back to Nohant and nursed him back to health. Their relationship remains one of the most romantic but mystifying ones in the history of French life.

Now there is a museum in Paris dedicated to her work, with papers and memorabilia from her celebrated life…photos, jewellery, letters, books, clothing, from Nohant as well as from her Paris home. Nohant is also a museum now and is open to the public during the summer months.

George Sand died nearly 150 years ago, but writers are still in awe at the volume of work she produced, even while caring for Chopin, her two children, and a country estate—which meant farming, with horses and other animals. She was a good horsewoman and enjoyed riding great distances, sometimes together with her house guests who would visit for lengthy stays…Flaubert, Victor Hugo, Liszt, and the Countess D'Agoult. Delacroix was a frequent guest, painting portraits of both of them, Chopin's now residing in the Louvre museum. She also had an open relationship with the poet Alfred de Musset with whom she travelled to Venice.

Le Procope is the oldest restaurant in Paris, frequented by George Sand, Balzac, Hugo and many other writers

George Sand used to frequent restaurants including Le Grand Véfour and the Tour d'Argent, as well as the left bank cafes around the Boulevard St. Michel. She writes that there was always a dinner after one of her plays, when she would take the actors for a meal and often would have a special banquet after a first night performance.

Chopin is buried in the Père Lachaise cemetery; George Sand was buried in the grounds of Nohant, just behind the tiny village church where her daughter Solange was married. It is said that it was Solange who was the cause of the break-up between Chopin and George even though Solange's husband carved the ornate statue of a weeping woman which is placed on the top of Chopin's grave. In the not infrequent quarrels between George and Solange, Chopin more often than not tended to support Solange.

Although George Sand is best remembered today by music-lovers as the mistress and patron of Frederic Chopin, in her own time she was a celebrity in her own right for her own achievements in literature rather than as an appendage to the musical genius. Her novels first drew attention of her contemporaries, then she became an outstanding success as a playwright, and then by insightful criticism of the government of her day, a significant force in the development of the French political system we see today. All in all, George Sand was not only the most creative woman of her generation, but also one of the outstanding European literary figures of the 19th century.

8

COLETTE—FRANCE'S GREATEST WOMAN AUTHOR

The two most famous denizens of the Palais Royal were Colette and Jean Cocteau. They were neighbours and could wave to each other from their windows. Colette liked to look at Cocteau in his low-ceilinged entresol apartment lit from below by the sunlight bouncing up from the pavement, as though he were an actor illuminated by footlights. Le Grand Véfour would have been one of their regular restaurants as it is situated in the Palais Royal and would have been a short walk for both of them—especially convenient if it was raining as they could walk through the arcades to get there.

Immobilized by arthritis, Colette seldom stirred from her bed during her last years. She'd sit under the shade she'd fashioned out of a piece of her signature blue writing paper, snug under her fur pelisses and attended by her faithful last—and much younger—husband.

Colette was full of contradictions. She despised feminists and said that the only things they deserved were the lash and the harem, but she herself divorced twice, lived openly as a lesbian for a decade, danced half-naked on the stage at the turn of the century and had an affair with her teenage stepson when she was approaching fifty. She turned her own mother into an endearing character, "Sido", and presented her to the public with convincing filial piety, but in real life she ignored her during her long decline and refused to attend her funeral. Colette was famously kind to cats and liked to picture herself as someone so close to nature she was almost feral, but in actuality she quite unnaturally rejected and ridiculed her own daughter, left her in the care of servants, then packed her off to strict boarding schools.

Finally, Colette's third and last husband was a Jew whom she adored and managed to save from harm during the Nazi Occupation, but she contributed to collaborationist magazines and in 1941 she published a novel, Julie de Carneilhan, full of anti-Semitic slurs. Chapters came out in Gringoire, a collaborationist review (in her issue there was a cartoon of "Uncle Sem" and one of of the Statue of Liberty wearing a menorah). And although she was quintessentially French and regarded as a national treasure, the Catholic Church refused to give her a religious funeral.

Of course, what this summary omits is her genius, which made many people want to forgive her all her shortcomings. She was generally considered to be the leading French woman novelist from the mid-1920s, when her talent emerged in all its glory, till her death at the age of eighty-one in 1954; now we would say she was, after the death of Proust in 1922, quite simply the most talented French novelist of her epoch, male or female. Although other writers, mostly male, spoke of her as an entirely unconscious writer guided only by her instincts, in fact Colette constantly revised her manuscripts, always searching for an exact, even shocking image.

Perhaps what confused critics was her originality. She claimed, with some justice, that she owed nothing to any preceding writer. In general French literature from the seventeenth century on has favoured short sentences, a narrow vocabulary of unremarkable words and a strict limit on metaphorical excess. Ironically, however, the two biggest literary figures of the century in France have turned out to be among the least characteristic—Proust and Colette. If Proust wrote extremely long sentences, unparalleled in contemporary French prose, Colette had an equally unidiomatic affection for strange words (she has the largest vocabulary in modern French) and for highly coloured imagery.

Along with Proust, Colette experimented with the first-person narrator, someone clearly based on herself but whom she both conceals and reveals in book after book and indisputably constructs. Like Proust, who used his narrator as a fil conducteur to draw us through his thousands of pages, Colette coquettishly suggests and subtracts details about herself in her entire nearly eighty-volume oeuvre of fiction, memoirs, journalism and drama.

The French today are slightly confused by how seriously English-speaking readers take Colette, a writer they think of as someone their grandmothers read under the hair-dryer (during her own lifetime she fared much better). Perhaps their under-valuation of Colette is linked to the fact that few women novelists, other than George Sand and Colette, dominated French literature in the long period before Yourcenar and Beauvoir; the French don't happen to have the equivalent to Jane Austen and George Eliot. Moreover, Colette's lurid image as one of those seedy old Decadents—friend to Rachilde (author of Monsieur Venus), Proust's mentor Robert de Montesquiou and the grandes cocottes Liane de Pougy and la Belle Otero, mistresses of kings—clings to her in her land of origin. That in her life-time she wrote constant articles for the press, posed for photographers as a mummy or a man, was whispered about in gossip columns, and even opened a chain of beauty salons (from which her clients emerged looking fifteen years older, according to Natalie Barney), all proved to her compatriots that she wasn't a serious person. Her case was analogous to that of Proust, who was dismissed at first because he had written about society events for Le Figaro.

In fact, one can make a good case that only foreigners can properly judge a con-temporary—distance gives the objectivity that time will eventually provide even to compatriots. Or, as the French sociologist and philosopher Pierre Bourdieu puts it more elegantly, "Foreign judgements are a little like the judgements of posterity." Just as the French were the first critics to praise Faulkner, just as Americans from the first admired Virginia Woolf and ignored her off putting Bloomsbury connections, in the same way Colette has always been esteemed in the English-speaking world more than at home.

For us, Colette is not only perverse, sometimes stern sensualist, she is also the great nature writer, who brings cats, dogs, plants, even the soil sharply into focus. And she is, in spite of herself, a feminist in the only way that makes sense in fic-tion—she shows a huge variety of women, victimized and monstrous, abject and proud, dependent and supremely resourceful. Even militant feminists have shown less of the range of female experience. Finally, she is the author of half a dozen masterpieces—Cheri and The Last of Cheri, The Pure and the Impure, Break of Day, My Mother's House and Sido—and the libretto for Ravel's exquis-ite one-act opera L'Enfant et les sortileges.

Colette—or, to give her her full name, Sidonie-Gabrielle Colette—was born on 28 January 1873 in the Burgundian village of St-Sauveur-en-Puisaye. Her mother, known as Sido or Sidonie, was a freethinker and atheist—not the usual French villager of the period. She had married a rich madman known in the region as the Ape. After his death she married a second time, for love—an amiable but spendthrift Captain Colette, who gradually dissipated the fortune she'd inherited from the Ape. The Captain was as kindly as he was impractical; his leg had been amputated in 1859 after a war wound, and in his later years he had what amounted to a sinecure; he was the tax collector of St-Sauveur.

But the family had its secrets. Sido's ancestors had converted to Protestantism in the seventeenth century and emigrated to Martinique, where they'd acquired slaves. Their children were biracial, a fact the family back in France hid by faking identity papers. Like Pushkin and Dumas, Colette turns out to be of mixed African descent (Colette herself was proud of her black heritage and frequently referred to it in letters to friends).

In the summer of 1889, when she was sixteen, Colette fell in love with a thirty-year-old writer and man-about-Paris, Henry Gauthier-Villars, known as Willy. He can be called a "writer" only in an honorary sense, given that he had a terrible lifelong writer's block and got the most famous composers of the day to pen his columns as a music critic and hired a team of ghost writers to churn out his many novels. He married the provocative, pretty and wildly clever Colette and soon enough set her to work ghosting "his" most famous novels, the Claudine series. Years later, when she was in her sixties and still nursing a grudge against her first husband, Colette claimed in her memoirs, My Apprenticeships, that she had never been so unhappy as with Willy, but her letters of the period belie her subsequent statements. Even she admitted that Willy had edited her work brilliantly; and from him she must have learned a lot about gender-bending, which would become her great subject. As her most recent biographer, Judith Thurman, puts it, "Colette's early work is a fascinating and baroque form of transvestism. She is a woman writing as a man, who poses as a boyish girl, Claudine, who marries a "feminized" man, the ageing Renaud, who pushes her into the arms of a female lover, Rezi, with whom she takes the virile role."

One aspect of Colette's life is how modern it sounds to today's reader. She ate sushi at the turn of the century, had a facelift in the 1920s, hired an acupuncturist, kept her wild hair permed her whole life, rejected religion, flouted most of society's rules—and ate with such relish and so little guilt that she ended up weighing 180 pounds. (Once, recovering from food poisoning, Colette soothed her stomach by downing a stuffed cabbage and a currant tart.) She announced that slimness was dangerously "masculinizing" women. She loved perfumes and sprayed each room with a different scent, attuned to its decor. She was one of the first serious writers to turn to the silent movies and devise scenarios that were neither novelistic nor theatrical but purely cinematic. She was obviously open to anything and everything; once when she had some painful dental work she asked, "Why can't one simply have one's teeth all pulled and replace them with green jade?"

Colette's second husband, Henry de Jouvenel, was a baron, the editor-in-chief of Le Matin and after the First World War France's chief delegate to the League of Nations. He was also the father of Colette's only child, Colette Renee de Jouvenel, who was born on 3 July 1913, when Colette was forty. Colette gave the baby the Provencal nickname her own father had given her—Bel-Gazou. Not for a moment did Colette let her child distract her from her work; as Colette observed with pride forgetting her objections to masculine women, "My strain of virility saved me from the danger which threatens the writer, elevated to a happy and tender parent, of becoming a mediocre author…" Not that Colette wasn't fiercely possessive of her daughter; once when the child fell and hurt herself, her mother slapped her and shouted, "I'll teach you to ruin what I made." A friend on another occasion had to tear a whip out of Colette's hand as she was about to lash her daughter. Bel-Gazou once announced she wanted to convert to Judaism because she'd observed that Jews love their children.

The daughter, of course, was the one who had to pay the price for her mother's fierce, complex feelings. Bel-Gazou grew up to be her mother's greatest disappointment—a spoiled brat, a bad student, later incapable of settling down to a career, chronically indecisive. When she eventually decided that she was a lesbian, her mother—who incidentally had lived ten years with another woman, the Marquise de Belbeuf, a transvestite better known as Missy—radiated disappointment. According to Colette's friend the novelist Michel del Castillo, "To be gay, in her view, showed a kind of sexual irresponsibility."

After Colette's death Bel-Gazou fought for years with her mother's last husband, Maurice Goudeket (who had been sixteen years younger than his wife), to gain control over the literary estate. Despite Colette's perfectly explicit preference for Maurice in her will, the daughter won—and turned herself into a high priestess of the cult of Colette. When she was sixty, eight years before her death, Bel-

Gazou recalled that her mother had been a font of "tenderness and warmth that made me radiant with happiness. And nothing that later came to torment or frustrate me could tarnish that magic."

The magic still radiates from Colette's apartment on the second floor of number 9 rue de Beaujolais. Today the place, which is just three rooms, belongs to the famous decorator Jacques Grange. I visited him there once to interview him, and he has kept a few of her things, including her portrait by Irving Penn—though he did remove from the ceiling the wallpaper Colette had put up so that when she was in bed she didn't have to look up at a harsh blank white rectangle. He can look down on the gardens of the Palais Royal from the window where Colette, crippled with arthritis, would survey her world.

9

THE FRENCH AT TABLE

Until the end of the Second World War, the wine growers of Beaujolais lived on the knife edge of poverty, and in bad years it was common for them to barter jugs of their wine for the essentials of life, the bread and cheese that were "the meat of the poor".

Little by little, a few inevitable things began happening, and the hand of destiny moved toward Beaujolais. Life became more expensive as postwar France grew wealthier. More people were drinking more wine of better quality, and vinification methods improved, suddenly giving passports to wines that used to spoil during travel. That happened at just the right time, because big new export markets opened up throughout the Common Market, Switzerland and Scandinavia and, soon after, in America and Canada and then Japan. Wine prices rose everywhere, but most dramatically for the "noble" Burgundies and Bordeaux. Beaujolais, on the other hand, remained what it always was: unpretentious, good, honest quality wine that could be had for a reasonable price.

The Parisians discovered it. Suddenly, in the middle sixties—just as the modern school of French gastronomy began coming into bloom—the bars and restaurants in the French capital that served the fashionable wine of the dynamic young crowd that would be called yuppies in America today, who enjoyed the good things in life but were too busy for three-hour lunches and too strapped to pay for heavyweight bottles of rare vintages. The traffic pattern of sales began curving more and more northward, away from Lyon and toward Paris, and then toward all points of the horizon. Restaurants were first opened in the late 1700's and the public were the first to see how the great places sought to attract customers, particularly in the centre of Paris.

As most travelers know, the tradition of whiling away hours in a Parisian café is well known. Most European cafes have their regular customers, but it is in Paris that the tradition is still kept alive. Meetings of writers, artists, philosophers, thinkers and revolutionaries once took place and perhaps still do. Most travelers watch the Parisians use their favourite café as a meeting place, at any time of day. They are the masters of making a coffee or a glass of wine last for hours. The most famous café, the Café de la Paix, is still considered the most historic, however not many Parisians are seen there unless they are visitors to the city. The place is too full of tourists hoping to see the writers and artists who have long since disappeared.

In France, lunch as well as dinner tend to be full-course meals with meat, vegetables, salad, cheese, dessert and wine and coffee. Coffee in France is served after the meal and usually costs extra. The French consider it barbaric to drink coffee during a meal and unless you order it with milk, it is served black. Parisians still enjoy dressing to go out for dinner even when dressing informally. If you want to be taken for a European don't wear jeans or sneakers. They will see you coming and put something extra on your bill for your sloppiness.

There are differences between a Brasserie, a Bistro, a café and baby bistros which are a spin off from deluxe restaurants where you can get a taste of a famous chef's cuisine without breaking the bank. A Brasserie usually has an Alsatian connection and that means lots of beer and Alsatian wines. A café is totally different. Not just a place for an aperitif, a coffee or croissant. Bistros are slowly disappearing because they are less expensive than restaurants but due to the high rents they can no longer afford to remain open.

The French have the fetes days—translated into English they are really just Bank holidays. But the French gather for a special dinner which is often as elaborate as a Christmas dinner. Guests will bring presents which can include food, or wine, sometimes a bottle often a case, flowers or a plant. Often when you go into a bakery to buy a cake the shop assistant will ask if its "pour offrir?—meaning are you going to offer it to some body...namely your host. The same applies in a florists you will get the same question—I always say yes, because then they gift wrap it and it looks terrific, even if it is only for yourself. The French know how to accept an invitation to dinner, often sending flowers or wine to you on the afternoon before the dinner. The English usually do it the other way round, sending flowers or a note after the event. One word of caution. If you are invited into a gracious

French home for dinner, be careful when you first sit down at the dinner table. Several times I have seen embarrassing moments when the guests are all seated—it happened to me once. The napkin or folded serviette beside you or in front of you often contains a bread roll hidden in its folds. You pick up the napkin to place on your knee, and away goes the bread roll across the floor. Quelle horreur! Why anyone would do that beats me, but beware.

The French at Table are certainly different when it comes to their choice of courses. The salad always comes after the main course because the salad dressing, or the vinegar in the dressing destroys the palate and is never served before the main dish. Then you must be aware not to have any strong martinis before dinner...very bad form because they also destroy your palate for the delicate flavours yet to come. Only a port or Dubonnet is acceptable, or champagne.

You will rarely be served butter with your bread, the French usually eat bread without it. The only time they do serve it is for breakfast to eat with a croissant and jam. Their omelettes are always good so don't miss one which is usually served with a salad and basket of freshly sliced baguette. The Croque Monsieur and Croque Madame are French creations rarely found outside France, and were very popular until the hamburger took over as an alternative snack.

10

LE GRAND VEFOUR

Table setting at the Grand Vefour restaurant

Le Grand Véfour was the successor to the Café de Chartres in the Palais Royal which had been started in 1784 and flourished under a succession of proprietors, surviving the Revolution, the Napoleonic period and the brief Allied occupation.

Jean Véfour was born in 1784, the same year as the opening of the Café de Chartres. At the age of thirty-six in 1820 he bought the Café de Chartres, a three-storey building with a kitchen on every floor. He decorated the rooms carefully and luxuriously, and developed an outstanding menu in which truffles figured conspicuously, as did fruits including grapefruit and gooseberries. A rival restaurant, opened by a man, not related but also called Véfour, motivated Jean Véfour to call his "Le 'Grand" Véfour" (the presumptuous upstart was soon bought out by yet another rival who did not try to capitalise on the Véfour name). The Grand Véfour became so profitable that he was able to retire three years later, he got married and sold the restaurant to his friend Louis Boissier who was a witness at his marriage. In his turn Boissier retired four years later in 1827. The Grand Véfour maintained its reputation and position as the most celebrated restaurant in Paris. Regular guests included Lamartine, Sainte-Beuve, George Sand, and Victor Hugo—who legend has it, ate more than was good for him.

Victor Hugo bust outside Comédie-Francaise

As we know, Hugo (1802-1885) was one of the most renowned figures in French literature. His two most famous novels, Les Miserables and The Hunchback of Notre Dame, were more famous than the plays he wrote. He always had severe critics who said that his accomplishments were just for the masses. They argued that his greatness was not because of well written work, but his genius for self promotion, patriotism, political courage and a huge output of work.

However other writers saw him as a 'visionary poet" who foresaw the future—a future in which democracy would replace monarchy or dictatorship—and judged his work as rivaling that of Goethe or Shelley. His poetry included his 'grief poetry' written about the accidental death of his daughter at a young age.

His writing for the theatre began when he was twenty-eight, he abandoned the theatre twelve years later. 'Hernani" was intended as a show piece of the new romantic spirit. The play was a great popular success, but most of the critics gave it terrible reviews, calling it ordinary, vulgar, absurd and incoherent. Parodies of it immediately appeared, but did nothing but to increase the publicity the play was already getting. Verdi also used the play for his opera 'Ernani" which is still performed today.

'Ruy Blas", Hugo's second most famous play, was not such a popular success but he papered the house with free tickets to students and they applauded when the older members of the audience booed. There were other plays with similar themes of love, jealousy, despair and most of them expressed his political lean-ings, the corruptibility of monarchies, the superiority of simple, honest folk. His play 'Le Roi s'amuse" was the foundation for Verdi's opera 'Rigoletto" however performances of the play were banned on the grounds that it was disrespectful of the monarchy.

His life was very dramatic and reads like one of his novels. Knowing there was a warrant out for his arrest in France, he fled the country to an island in the English channel. His sons who had been imprisoned were released in 1852 and his wife and daughter left him to return to France. His political views had forced him into exile. as soon as the empire fell, he hastened back to France and even tried to vol-unteer for combat against the Prussians.

And on one of the tables in the Grand Véfour restaurant, there lies a plaque in Hugo's memory.

Statue of Honoré de Balzac, Ave de Friedland

Another frequent guest at the restaurant was Balzac, one of the great masters of the French novel. While hard at work on a book, he would don a a monk's robe and make a point of practically fasting, allowing himself only a dinner of consommé, steak, salad and a glass of water, and at other times small portions of fruit and eggs. But once finished, he was known to devour huge quantities of food, on one occasion polishing off "a hundred Ostend oysters, twelve cutlets of salt-meadow mutton, a duck with turnips, two partridges and a Normandy sole," on top of desserts, fruit and liqueurs he would finish up with.

The author was said to have an encyclopaedic interest in the culinary arts, with the cycle of La Comédie Humaine containing some 15 different kinds of fish and 16 kinds of fruit, as well as countless meals eaten by parvenu shopkeepers or lawyers. He held dinner parties based around gastronomic themes, at one time serving a meal of nothing but onions: onion soup, his favourite onion puree, onion juice, onion fritters and onions with truffles. The intent was to demonstrate the vegetable's cleansing aspects—which it did: all his guests became ill!

Balzac appreciated a restaurant like the Grand Véfour because it masterfully combined his two favourite passions—literature and gastronomy—in a way that nourished both the body and the soul. Its existence, however, was threatened as early as 1830, when the quarter slowly fell into decline. Thankfully, Sainte-Beuve, Lamartine and, more particularly, Hugo came to its rescue, guided by their love of fine cuisine. Still, Le Grand Véfour would often change hands, and even had to endure the "disgrace" of offering paper napkins.

Eventually the location would become unfashionable, with the result that in 1905 the restaurant had to close, becoming a chess club. After the First World War, in 1920 the facade of the building was declared a historic site by the authorities.

After the Second World War, the proprietor of Maxim's, Louis Vaudable, bought the building and moved Maxim's there, as its original location had been shut down by the military authorities. However in spite of his best efforts, Vaudable was unable to save the restaurant and sold it to Raymond Oliver, who reopened it under its old name in 1948 with a new menu deriving from Oliver's provincial origin. This time the restaurant was an outstanding success, being patronised by Colette and Jean Cocteau who attended the opening, followed by the great names of the artistic and literary worlds, including Jean Giraudoux, Sacha Guitry, Louis Aragon, Jean-Paul Sartre, Simone de Beauvoir, Marcel Pagnol, Juliette Greco, Jean Genet etc. Since then we have had the era of the star chefs, and to the Grand Véfour came kings and queens, celebrities from the worlds of politics, fashion, haute couture and finance.

In December 1983 a bomb exploded in the restaurant, seriously wounding several patrons and virtually destroying the interior. The restaurant was then bought by Jean Taittinger, who spent a fortune and several years restoring the interior, reopened the famous restaurant with a new look and a new "neo-classic" menu.

11

THE DIVINE SARAH

Sarah Bernhardt is considered one of the greatest actresses of all time. The scandal over her behaviour and life style are legendary as well as tours around the world. Australia, America, South America and the U. K.

The actress was always her own master. She earned her own living, and owned her own theatre In this theatre her dressing room was actually an apartment which can still be visited today.

She was a sickly child and because she suffered with a persistent cough, it was thought that she would die early from consumption. Death became a kind of obsession with her and there is the well known story that she often slept in a coffin which she purchased early in life.

One evening she was taken to the Comédie-Française to see her first real play "When the curtain slowly rose I thought I was going to faint", she recorded in her memoirs. "It was, in fact, the curtain of my life which was rising" (My Double Life)

Sarah was born on October 23rd 1844. Her mother Judith was 16 then, a courtesan by profession, the identity of Sarah's father in uncertain. Sarah was sent off to Brittany where she was raised by a peasant couple, the wife being a nurse and the father an unemployed disabled invalid. And accident in Sarah's infancy resulted in severe burns and the first of many injuries to her knees. Judith, then in Belgium, was notified and returned to France to take care of Sarah until she recovered, at which time Judith moved Sarah and her foster-parents to Paris, where Sarah lived for the next five years.

The foster-father died, his wife remarried, and moved from the Paris apartment, but was unable to notify Judith, not being able to write. A surprise encounter with Judith's sister Rosine, also a courtesan, resulted in an unfortunate accident to Sarah, who suffered fractures of one of her arms and a kneecap. Judith again returned to look after Sarah during her convalescence which lasted for the next two years. During this time Judith gave birth to another daughter, Jeanne.

At age 8 Sarah could neither read, write nor count. She was sent to a boarding school which she liked, but was subject to violent spells of rage which caused short bouts of illness. She then transferred to an aristocratic convent boarding school, Notre Dame de Grandchamp, her admission there required the influence of the Duc de Morny, one of Judith's patrons. Sarah enjoyed being at this school also, though rarely visited by her mother or other family members. She went through a religious phase there and was obsessed with the idea of her death.

15 was the age at which a girl could legally marry, however Sarah had no desire to marry anyone. A family conference was held at which the Duc de Morny observed that Sarah had theatrical talent and should be sent to the Conservatoire of Music and Drama, supposed to be the finest drama school in the world. Due again to his influence she was accepted and stayed happily for the next two years, and at graduation won 2nd prize for comedy.

Morny again pulled strings and got her an interview with Edouard Thierry, administrator of the Comédie-Française, who took her on as a "pensionnaire". After doing poorly in her debut performance, a row erupted at a celebration of Molière's birthday, to which Sarah took her little sister Regina. Regina happened to stand on the train of a very large obese societaire who grabbed her and shoved her against a pillar, causing a gash in Regina's forehead which bled furiously. Sarah nataurally was enraged and slapped the massive actress so hard that she stumbled and fell to the floor. At the insistence of the veteran actress, Sarah was not given any parts to play unless she apologised and paid a fine, neither of which Sarah was prepared to do. After a few weeks of this impasse, Sarah's contract was terminated by the Comédie-Française. This was in 1862, she was 18.

She then got a job at the Gymnase theatre, which put on mostly popular light comedies. Sarah appeared in a few of these but was not satisfied and quit the Gymnase. She then decided to go travelling, had various love affairs, including one in Belgium with Henri, the Prince de Ligne, whom she later described as the

"Love of her Life", and became pregnant by him. She returned to Paris, living in an apartment on the Rue Duphot with her sister Regina and Mme. Guerard. She gave birth to her son Maurice on Decmber 22nd 1864. She was twenty.

The next most important theatre in Paris after the Comédie-Française was the Odeon, where in addition to the classics of the French repertory, newer plays were produced. With the help of the French minister of the arts, she got an interview with one of the Managers of the Odeon, Felix Duquesnel who was charmed by her, and employed her at a salary of 150 francs a month. Her first roles were not suitable, but them she was an outstanding success as Cordelia in King Lear, then as the female lead in "Kean", by Alexandre Dumas. She also starred in two plays by George Sand, who became one of her friends though Sand was then in her sixties. However she the most successful in the sentimental romantic play "Le Passant" by Coppee in the role of Zanetto, a young male troubadour, which merited a "royal command" performance at the Tuileries palace following the invitation of the Emperor Napoleon 3rd in 1868.

The Franco-Prussian war broke out in 1870; Paris was besieged by the Prussian army, so Sarah sent her children and her mother Judith to Hamburg for safety, while she herself opened a hospital at the Odeon theatre, where she and Mme. Guerard were nurses, for which she received a medal from a grateful government.

Sarah recovered her children and mother and took them both back to Paris near the end of the war. However when the war was over, a kind of civil war broke out in Paris with the "Commune" trying to take over the government. This ended in 1871.

Sarah then returned to the refurbished Odeon theatre in 1872, where she had outstanding success in Victor Hugo's play "Ruy Blas" as the Queen of Spain. The opening was attended by the Prince of Wales and by Victor Hugo. She was then invited by the Comédie-Française to them, which she did, thus breaking her contract with the Odeon, which sued her and she was forced to pay a huge fine. She had by then become a subject of constant coverage by the press, which showered her with both good and bad publicity. He beloved younger sister Regina died in 1874 after a long illness.

She took up painting and sculpture, which sold well, painting not so well. She built a house in 1872, acted leads with the leading man Mounet-Sully in Phedre in December of 1874, and in Hugo's Hernani in 1877. She would take a balloon ride, and then end up in a row over it with Perrin (the manager of Comédie-Française), who threatened to fine her, while she threatened to quit.

During a tour of London, the impresario Edward Jarrett got her to sign a contract to perform in private houses in London, which paid well, and resulted in a very successful and profitable tour in London. She rented a house in Chester Square, stayed there with Mme Guerard for six weeks, acting in two Molière plays and Phedre. There was extensive publicity, and on top of her acting accomplishments, she managed to sell sculptures and paintings at an art gallery which the Prince of Wales and the Prime Minister Gladstone attended.

On her return to Paris, she came into conflict again with Perrin, and resigned from the Comédie-Française, over an alleged breach of contract, which saw her lose her investment in the pension fund, get fined 100, 000 Francs, and the ensuing lawsuits carried on for twenty years. She returned to the Gaiety theatre in London, which let her chose her own roles. The Comédie-Française wanted her back, but she refused, going instead to Brussels and Copenhagen, and then Jarrett got her to sign a contract for her first American tour, giving her the choice of 8 plays and the actors, at a huge salary plus expenses for personal maids, costumes etc. This tour was an enormous success.

In August, when theatres closed, Sarah would leave for her home off the coast of Brittany. She took a ship for Belle Isle. As she crossed the drawbridge of the house, a servant unfurled from the flagstaff her personal self-designed standard. Up at six, she would don fisherman's clothes and a white beret, sling a gun over her shoulder and, accompanied by two huge mastiffs and a black servant boy, hurry to the beach to shoot duck.

Lunch at one was served on Quimper plates. Sarah ate sparingly, mainly caviar, oysters and sorbets, but insisted on sampling each course and, if it was not perfect, would summon the cooks and berate them publicly. In the afternoon there would be tennis or shrimping, or perhaps the reception of a visiting dignitary, on one occasion King Edward VII. When storms almost wiped out the Belle Isle fishing fleet in 1911, it was Bernhardt who organized a theatrical gala and sent the proceeds to be distributed among the needy. Money for Sarah meant gold in a chamois bag or brass-bound strongbox, easy to give or spend, and so despite huge earnings all her life, she was on the verge of financial ruin. Evenings were given over to cards, dominoes or a performance by a guest.

During her first American tour in 1883-84, Bernhardt travelled on special trains with her own private carriage. All expenses were paid except for her costumes which she bought at great financial cost. Her arrival in New York was a media event with speeches, flowers and throngs of reporters, she stayed at a fashionable hotel on 5th Avenue. Her theatrical debut in New York was in the play Adrienne Lecouvreur, her most successful however was in "La Dame aux Camillias".

Boston was even better, where the audiences were more cultivated, some spectators even able to speak French, and she was entertained by members of Boston society in their homes, in contrast to New York. Some unfortunate publicity over a stupid incident with a fishing-fleet owner caused her to leave Boston; she went to Montreal where the Roman Catholic archbishop forbade his congregations to attend immoral French plays by an immoral French actress—a decree which assured her success in Montreal, particularly among the young.

Next to Chicago, where a similar attitude on the part of the Episcopal bishop led to a similar result. Then followed a long, tiring tour including many one-night engagements, visiting New Orleans; Mobile, Alabama; Atlanta; Memphis; Cincinnati; Detroit; Pittsburgh; Toronto; Washington D. C. ; Baltimore; and Philadelphia, before ending back in New York for a big send-off on the liner America. The tour was a financial success, earning for her the equivalent of a million dollars in today's money.

She returned to Paris where a flood of spiteful publicity denied the success of the American tour. She endured a few weeks of this, then returned to London for the start of a long and highly applauded European tour. Somewhere in Europe she met Aristidis (self-named Jean) Damala, the son of a rich Greek shipping magnate, who was then a rather dashing army officer, handsome, arrogant, a womaniser, would-be actor, a gambler and drug-addict. She fell madly in love with him, her friends were mystified not knowing what she could see in him and told her so, but in spite of that she decided to marry. On account of religious differences—he Greek Orthodox, she Roman Catholic—they could not be married in France, but in England where she and Damala were married on April 4th 1882, when she was 38, he 28. Her son Maurice was hostile to Damala and bitter about the marriage.

At that point, in the autumn of 1882, Victorien Sardou wrote a play "Fedora" for her, but refused to allow Damala to act in it. To save the feelings of her son and of Damala, she bought a theatre, the Ambigu, appointed Maurice manager and Damala her leaading man. Both choices were unfortunate: Damala, not even a good actor, was piling up debts for drugs and other women; Maurice was mismanaging the theatre. Constant rows led Damala to leave her, and he went off to America with the intention of joining the army there.

Sarah was herself in debt, and in 1883 went on a tour of Scandinavia accompanied by her playwright lover Jean Richepin. On their return to Paris she found Damala living in her house, but the continuation of his drug taking and gambling led to a legal separation at Sarah's instigation; Damala then took up acting again.

Richepin wrote a series of plays for her which were put on at the Ambigu but failed miserably. Sardou once again came to her rescue with a play called "Theodora" for her with lots of Byzantine costumes and sets, which had long runs in Paris and London, 300 performances in Paris and more than 100 in London.

In 1886, her manager, the impresario Jarrett, arranged a tour of south and central America followed by a tour of the eastern United States. She toured for 13 months on that occasion. On her return voyage across the Atlantic she fell and seriously injured her right knee which gave her trouble for the next 20 years. A lucrative tour of the British Isles was followed by her return to Paris where she bought a big house at 56 Boulevard Pereire, which was her principal home for the rest of her life.

In November 1887 she played in Sardou's Tosca which got poor reviews but an enthusiastic popular following. The same year her son Maurice married a Polish princess, Terka Jablonska, very much with the approval of Sarah.

In the Spring of 1888, Sarah embarked on a 12-month tour of Europe including Egypt and Russia. Back in Paris in March 1889, she found Damala ill, she took him to her house and when he was sufficiently recovered had him as her leading man in "La Dame aux Camellias", but after a six-week run he collapsed and was taken to hospital where he died on April 18th 1889, at the age of thirty-four.

Sarah was then 45. In the same year Maurice's wife gave birth to their first daughter, Simone.

In 1890 Sarah starred in one of her most famous roles, Jeanne d'Arc; the run was cut short after sixteen weeks, however, on account of her recurrent knee trouble which caused her agony. She recovered enough later, though, to play in London for the summer season, and in October in Sardou's Cleopatra. 1891 saw her undertake a world tour, including Australia, New Zealand, Hawaii, Samoa, the Americas, all over Europe, returning home in September 1893—richer by three and a half million Francs!

She had bought property on a small island off the coast of Brittany, called Belle Isle en Mer, before her world tour, securing a hotel being built there and turning it into a grand house for herself, as well as building several guest houses for her friends to stay in. She spent the next thirty summers there.

Also in 1893 she took over the management of the Renaissance theatre and ran it for the next five years. In January 1889 she bought the Nations theatre renamed it the Sarah-Bernhardt theatre, built a spacious apartment in it, where she gave dinner parties for her friends between matinee and evening performances. Her roles there included Hamlet and the lead in Rostand's play "L'Aiglon". In 1905–6 a "final American tour" of America took place followed by three more final American tours.

When she was seventy and still playing leading roles, the various aspects of her life since 1900 came together, although soon her leg would have to be amputated and replaced with an artificial limb. The Government decided to put their seal on the public's acclaim. Protocol did not allow them to honour her as an actress, but in recognition of her services as a nurse in the 1870–71 war and as a purveyor of French civilization abroad, Sarah Bernhardt received the scarlet ribbon of the order established by the Emperor Napoleon, the Legion d'Honneur.

Sarah's Farewell

Who's done Camille in ev'ry clime
From here to Zanzibar
And trickled briny tears enough
To float a man-o'-war?

Who did it when our grandma was
A lassie blithe and gay?
Who'll still be doing it no doubt
When Baby Doll is gray?
Who needs but pack her gladsome rags
And hit the farewell trail
Whene'er the treasurer reports
She's running out of kale?
Who slips it o'er in perfect French,
Assures US that it's art,
And hauls our Yankee shekels
From the show-shop in a cart?
Who makes us say "How wonderful!"
And "Mabel, ain't it fine!"
And wonder what it's all about?
Why, Bernhardt the Divine!

—Cornelia Otis Skinner

12

GEORGE FEYDEAU

George Feydeau is the French playwright who has been referred to as "the greatest of a great age of French farceurs and the first to enter the modern repertory". Feydeau did his best to make France laugh through his vaudevillian farces and, in the process, dominated the genre well into La Belle Epoque of the nascent twentieth century, long regarded as a golden time of beauty, innovation, and peace between France and its European neighbors.

George Feydeau was born in Paris in 1862 to Lodzea Stewska, a Polish woman, and Ernest-Aimé Feydeau, a prolific but unsuccessful novelist, although George was rumoured at various points to actually be the son of the Duke of Morny or Napoleon III. His father Ernest counted a number of other French writers among his friends, including the poet Charles Baudelaire and the novelist Gustave Flaubert. Ernest's best known work was Fanny (1858); he was also known for an archeological study titled History of Funeral Customs and Graves of Ancient Peoples (1862).

George was only eleven when his father died in 1873; his mother married drama critic Henri Gouquier, and the couple promptly sent George to a boarding school, the Lycee Saint-Louis, where the young man soon earned a reputation for laziness. He developed a career as an amateur actor of sorts, penning various skits and sketches to entertain his fellow classmates and to avoid homework. He wrote his first comic monologue Through the Window (Par la fenêtre) at the age of twenty, and various light single-act plays, which drew praise from critics, but poor sales. He continued writing during a year of military duty, then turned to earning his living as a racing correspondent.

On the Boulevards of Paris, however, Feydeau was a hit, with his dashing figure, good looks, and wavy chestnut hair. He charmed many a woman, both before and following his marriage at 27 to Marianne Duran, heiress and daughter of Carolus-Duran, a well known—and well-off—portrait painter who took care of Feydeau's immediate financial concerns. Their partnership was likely a challenging one, though, given George's domestic habit of remaining in bed until well into the afternoon, then departing the house at six for his aperitif at the Café Napolitain, followed by an evening meal at Maxim's, not returning home until three of four in the morning, only to resume the same routine the next day.

It was at Maxim's that Feydeau would spend many an evening at his permanently reserved table, taking in the night life crowd—an eclectic mix of upper-class Parisian society, from the nouveaux riches to the gigolos and kept women, as well as artists, bookmakers, journalists, politicians, con men and detectives. The goings-on would typically be accompanied by the sounds of a gypsy orchestra playing Paul Delmet's sentimental tunes and the popping of champagne corks. The walls covered with mirrors only added to the intensity of the atmosphere, and what Feydeau observed there would become the stuff of his later farces.

In fact, the Feydeau classic light, farcical comedy, The Lady from Maxim's (La Dame de chez Maxim, 1899), is named after the restaurant. The comedy revolves around "The Shrimp", a notorious dancer from the Moulin Rouge, whom Doctor Lucien Petypon, a young married man, picks up on a wild evening of debauchery and brings home. The woman is discovered in Petypon's bed by the young man's uncle, General Petypon du Grele, just home from a long stint in Africa, and who mistakes The Shrimp for the doctor's wife. This forces the doctor to pass the woman off as Madame Petypon at his niece's wedding reception at a chateau in Touraine, where her every word and action—no matter how vulgar or outrageous—is taken as the height of fashion by the provincial ladies, simply because she hails from Paris.

La Puce a l'Oreille—That Starts Me Thinking—also combines mistaken identities, misunderstandings, and double entendres to form a dizzying series of madcap mix-ups. The play follows the antics of a Mrs. Chandebise as she deals with her nagging suspicion—a "flea in her ear"—that her husband is up to no good at a seedy hotel. This wildly farcical maison de passe has customers escaping unwelcome intruders by pushing a button that swings round one entire wall of the room, transferring them to the adjoining bedroom and bringing the guest of that room on to the stage. What follows is a comedy of disguises, confusions, misapprehensions, revelations, panics, bruised egos, and even attempted murder. The farce depends on split-second timing, so Paris's stage mechanics were evidently on the mend.

1883 saw Feydeau, now 24, work as secretary to the Renaissance Theatre, where he wrote his first successful play, Tailleur pour dames (Ladies' Tailor) which enjoyed a successful run at the theatre. Feydeau would later take a break in writing in order to study authors who had succeeded in farce, including Eugène Labiche, Henri Meilhac, and Alfred Hennequin. The result was Champignol in Spite of Himself (Champignol malgré lui, 1892) and Monsieur Has Gone Hunting (Monsieur chasse!, 1892), the first of which became a major success at the Nouveautés after having been rejected by the Palais-Royal. From then on, it was one success followed by another, and by 1894, three of his farces were running simultaneously in Paris: Un Fil à la Patte (On a String), Le Ruban (The Ribbon) and L'Hôtel du Libre-Échange (Hôtel Paradiso). His career continued to blossom as he became the most popular playwright of the boulevard theatre and a great success abroad as well. Sometimes his plays were performed in foreign language translation before they were performed in France.

Contrasting Feydeau to one of his immediate predecessors, Courteline, it is clear that his originality shines through in several ways. His farces are more quickly-paced, reflecting the accelerated mood in Paris at the time, fueled by the advent of electricity, telephones and cars. His work also displays a complexity seen elsewhere in the arts. The French author Alfred Capus was of the view that dramatists faced a unique challenge in chronicling the society of his day because, "to use a metaphor from photography, it will never sit still long enough to be snapped".

Feydeau's plays are also distinguished by their warmth. Courteline's Boubouroche (1893), for example, is a cruel comedy about a naïve sentimental petit bourgeois, who is throughly tricked by his girlfriend, who ends up believing her lies. Feydeau, on the other hand, celebrates sentiment, and when he places someone in absurd circumstances, it is in order to laugh *with* them rather than *at* them. For example, "Leonie Early" is about a woman faking a pregnancy who, with the support of her mother and midwife, asks her husband to put a chamber pot on his head. He initially declines but, after being told that satisfying his pregnant wife's wishes would be in the interests of the child, agrees to crown himself with the chamber pot—which then becomes stuck on his head!

Among Feydeau's most versatile props are beds, which he had actors sleep in, hide in, and bounce on. Beds also played an increasingly important role in Feydeau's private life, which was miserable despite his public successes. He had a propensity for womanizing, nightlife, and gambled incessantly on the stock exchange, a habit that left him perpetually in debt. Instead of building his own personal fortune, his plays only served to rescue him from penury, and by 1903, he was forced to sell his valuable collection of Impressionist art works just to pay the bills.

All of this naturally placed strains on his marriage to Marianne, and in 1909, a violent quarrel between the two of them led Feydeau to move to the Hôtel Terminus, near the Gare Saint-Lazare, where he surrounded himself with his paintings, his books, and some 250 perfumes. As the rising young playwright, Lucien Guitry's son Sacha, was to put it, the burdens of marriage are too heavy to be borne by two people alone.

Commenting on the change in Paris theatre since the fin de siecle social realism as practised by Octave Mirabeau and various followers of Zola, the theatre critic of the Revue des Deux Mondes wrote in 1905:

> *"Everyone knows that one of the dominant tendencies in today's theatre is optimism. After being down in the dumps for a decade our theatre paints life in rosy colours. It portrays only nice characters, generous souls, motivated by tact and unselfishness, simple yet noble."*

By 1916, Feydeau's health and mind had begun to deteriorate from the effects of syphilis and in 1919, he declared he was Napoleon III, at which point friends and family committed him to a sanatorium in Ruel-Malmaison, where he died in 1921.

Twenty years later, his play, Madam's Late Mother (Feu la mère de madame), became part of the Comédie-Française's repertory, soon to be joined by some of his other plays, thus establishing him as a modern "classic."
To some, Feydeau is seen as a precursor of Dadaism, surrealism, and the absurd. Perhaps Norman Shapiro, author of the book Four Farces by George Feydeau (U. of Chicago, 1970), best summarized his contributions in the Times Literary Supplement of June 18, 1971, where he writes of the grandeur found in Fey-

deau's compositions, in spite of their levity and seeming triviality, and in his ultimate canonical designation of the dramatist as "the Bach of his genre."

13

ISADORA DUNCAN, BRICKTOP, AND MAURICE CHEVALIER

ISADORA DUNCAN (1877–1927)

Isadora Duncan arrived in Paris in 1905 from San Francisco. She wrote her autobiography in 1927 which tells of her arrival and struggles after arriving in France. She was determined to bring her new style of dancing to Europe. Adam Gopnick, in his book about Americans in Paris, writes that "she was a kind of dancing bridge between the awed bougeois fascination with France of the Wharton-James era and the coming avant-garde wave of the Stein-Hemingway generation." Her younger brother and sister were in Paris with her which seemed to help her when she first arrived. After her death, her brother Raymond stayed on in Paris and continued the school they had founded there. Here is an extract from her autobiography.

MY LIFE

"There was always a deficit between our expenditure and our earnings, but it was a period of peace. But this peaceful atmosphere had made Raymond restless. He left for Paris and in the spring he bombarded us with telegrams imploring us to come to Paris, so one day Mother and I packed up our belongings and took the Channel boat.

After the fogs of London we arrived on a spring morning at Cherbourg. France seemed to us like a garden and from Cherbourg to Paris we leaned out of our third-class window all the way. Raymond met us at the station. He had let his hair grow long over his ears, and wore a turned-down collar and a flowing tie. We were somewhat astonished at this metamorphosis but he explained to us that this was the fashion of the Latin Quarter where he lived. He took us to his lodging where we met a little midinette running down the stairs, and he regaled us on a bottle of red wine which, he said, cost thirty centimes. After the red wine we set out to look for a studio. Raymond knew two words of French and we walked along the streets saying "Chercher atelier". What we did not know was that atelier does not only mean a studio in France, but any kind of workshop. Finally, at dusk we found a studio in a courtyard, at the extraordinary price of fifty francs a month, furnished. We were overjoyed, and paid a month in advance. We could not imagine why it was so cheap, but that night we found out! Just as we had composed ourselves to rest, terrific earthquakes seemed to shake the studio and the whole thing seemed to jump into the air and then fall flat. This was repeated over and over again. Raymond went down to inspect and found that we were refuged over a night imprimerie. Hence the cheapness of the studio. It somewhat damped our spirits but, as fifty francs meant a great deal to us in those days, I proposed that it sounded like the sea and that we should pretend that we were at the seaside. The concierge provided the meals, twenty-five centimes for lunch and one franc a head for dinner, including wine. She used to bring up a bowl of salad and say with a polite smile, "Il faut tourner la salade, Monsieur et Mesdames, il faut tourner la salade."

Raymond gave up the midinette and devoted himself to me and we used to get up at five o'clock in the morning, such was our excitement at being in Paris, and begin the day by dancing in the gardens of the Luxembourg, walk for miles all over Paris and spend hours in the Louvre. Raymond had already got a portfolio of drawings of all the Greek vases, and we spent so much time in the Greek vase room that the guardian grew suspicious and when I explained in pantomime that I had only come there to dance, he decided that he had to do with harmless lunatics, so he let us alone. I remember we spent hours and hours sitting on the waxed floor, sliding about to see the lower shelves, or standing on tip-toe saying, "Look, here is Dionysus," or "Come here, here's Medea killing her children."

Day after day we returned to the Louvre, and could hardly be forced to leave at closing time. We had no money, we had no friends in Paris, but we wanted nothing. The Louvre was our Paradise, and I have since met people who saw us then—me in my white dress and Liberty hat, and Raymond in his large black hat, open collar and flowing tie—and say we were two bizarre figures, so young and so absolutely absorbed in the Greek vases. At the closing hour we walked back through the dusk, lingering before the statues in the Tuileries gardens, and when we had dined off white beans, salad and red wine, we were about as happy as anyone could be.

Raymond was very clever with his pencil. In a few months he had copied all the Greek vases in the Louvre. But there exist certain silhouettes, which were afterwards published, which were not from Greek vases at all, but me, dancing in the nude, photographed by Raymond, which were passed off as Greek vases.

Besides the Louvre, we visited the Cluny Museum, the Carnavelet Museum, and Notre Dame. and all the other museums of Paris. I was especially entranced by the Carpeau group before the Opera, and the Rude on the Arc de Triomphe. There was not a monument before which we did not stand in adoration, our young American souls uplifted before this culture which we had striven so hard to find.

Spring lengthened into summer and the great Exhibition of 1900 was opened, when, to my great joy, but to the discomfiture of Raymond, Charles Halle appeared one morning at our studio in the Rue de la Gaiete. He had come over to see the Exhibition, and after that I was his constant companion. And I could not have had a more charming or intelligent guide. All day we roamed through the buildings and in the evening we dined at the Eiffel Tower. He was kindness itself, and when I was tired he would put me into a rolling chair, and I was often tired, for the art of the Exhibition did not seem to me at all equal to the art of the Louvre, but I was very happy, for I adored Paris and I adored Charles Halle.

On Sundays we took a train and went into the country, to wander through the gardens of Versailles or the forest of Saint-Germain. I danced for him in the forest, and he made sketches of me. And so the summer passed. It was not so happy, of course, for my poor mother and Raymond.

One great impression remained with me of the Exhibition of 1900—the dancing of Sadi Yacca, the great tragic dancer of Japan. Night after night Charles Halle and I were thrilled by the wondrous art of this great tragedian.

Another, even greater impression, that has remained with me all my life, was the "Rodin Pavillon," where the complete works of the wonderful sculptor were shown for the first time to the public. When I first entered this Pavillon I stood in awe before the work of the great master. Without, at that time, knowing Rodin, I felt that I was a new world, and each time I came I was indignant at the vulgar people who said "Where is his head?" or "Where is her arm?" I often turned and apostrophised the crowd, rating them soundly. "Don't you know," I used to say, "that this is not the thing itself, but a symbol—a conception of the ideal of life."

Autumn approached, and the last days of the Exhibition. Charles Halle had to return to London, but before going he presented to me his nephew, Charles Noufflard. "I leave Isadora in your care." he said, when he was going. Noufflard was a young man of about twenty-five, more or less blase, but he was completely captivated by the naiveté of this little American girl who had been confided to his care. He set out to complete my education in French art, telling me much about the Gothic, and making me appreciate for the first time the epochs of Louis XIII, XIV, XV and XVI.

We had left the studio in the Rue de la Gaiete and, with the remainder of our little savings, we took a large studio in the Avenue de Villiers. Raymond arranged this studio in a most original manner. Taking sheets of tin foil, he rolled them and placed them over the gas jets, allowing the gas to flare through them like old Roman torches, thereby considerably increasing our gas bills!

In this studio my mother revived her music and, as in our childhood's days, for hours and hours she would play Chopin, Schumann and Beethoven. We had no bedroom or a bathroom in our studio. Raymond painted Greek columns round the walls and we had a few carved chests in which we kept our mattresses. At night we took them from the chests and slept upon them. At this time Raymond invented his famous sandals, having discovered that all shoes were obnoxious. He was of an inventive disposition and he spent three-quarters of the night working out his inventions and hammering, while my poor mother and I had to sleep on the chests as best we could.

Charles Noufflard was a constant visitor and one day he brought to our studio two of his comrades, a pretty youth called Jacques Beaugnies, and a young literary man called Andre Beaunier. Charles Noufflard was very proud of me and delighted to show me to his friends, as a phenomenal American product. Naturally I danced for them. I was then studying the music of Chopin's Preludes, Waltzes and Mazurkas. My mother played extremely well, with the firm, strong touch of a man, and with great feeling and insight, and she would accompany me for hours. It was then that Jacques

Beaugnies had the idea of asking his mother, Madame de St. Marceau, the wife of the sculptor, to have me dance one evening for her friends.

Mme. de St. Marceau had one of the most artistic and chic salons in Paris and a rehearsal was arranged in the studio of her husband. At the piano sat a most remarkable man, with the fingers of a wizard. I was instantly attracted to him.

"Quel ravissement!" he exclaimed, "quel charme! Quelle jolie enfant!" And, taking me in his arms he kissed me on both cheeks, in French fashion. He was Messager, the great composer.

The evening of my debut arrived. I danced before a group of people so kind, so enthusiastic, that I was quite overcome. They scarcely waited for the end of a dance to call out, "Bravo, bravo, comme elle est exquise! Quel enfant!" and at the end of the first dance a tall figure, with piercing eyes, rose and embraced me.

"Quel est ton nom, petite fille?" he asked.

"Isadora," I replied.

"Mais ton petit nom?"

"When I was a little girl they called me Dorita."

"Oh, Dorita," he cried, kissing my eyes, my cheeks and my mouth, "tu es adorable," and then, Madame de St. Marceau took my hand and said, "This is the great Sardou."

In fact that room held all who counted in Parisian life, and, when I left, covered with flowers and compliments, my three cavaliers, Noufflard, Jacques Beaugnies and Andre Beaunier, escorted me home beaming with pride and satisfaction because their little phenomenon had been such a success.

Of these three young men the one who was to become my greatest friend was not the tall and pleasant Charles Noufflard, or the good-looking Jacques Beaugnies, but the rather under-sized pale-faced Andre Beaunier. He was pale and round-faced and wore glasses, but what a mind! I was always a "cerebrale", and although people will not believe it, my love affairs of the head, of which I had many, were as interesting to me as those of the heart. Andre, who was at that time writing his first books, "Petrarch" and "Simonde", came every day to see me, and it was through him that I became acquainted with all the finest French literature.

By this time I had learned to read and converse fairly easily in French, and Andre Beaunier would read aloud to me in our studio for long afternoons and evenings. His voice had a cadence in it that was exquisitely sweet. He read to me the works of Molière, Flaubert, Theophile Gautier, Maupassant, and it was he who first read to Maeterlinck's "Pelleas et Melisande" and all the modern French books of the day.

Every afternoon there was a timid knock at the door of the studio. It was Andre Beaunier, always with a new book or magazine under his arm. My mother could not understand my enthusiasm for this man, who was not her beau ideal of what a lover should be, for, as I have said before, he was fat and small with small eyes and one had to be a "cerebrale" to understand that those eyes were sparkling with wit and intelligence. Often, when he had read to me for two or three hours, we went off on the top of a Seine 'bus and rode down to the Ile de la Cite to gaze at Notre Dame in the moonlight. He knew every figure of the facade and could tell me the history of every stone. Then we would walk home and now and then I would feel the timid pressure of Andre's fingers on my arm. On Sundays too, we would take a train and go out to Marly. There is a scene in one of Beaunier's books in which he describes these walks in the forest—how I used to dance before him down the paths beckoning to him like a nymph or dryad bubbling with laughter.

He confided to me all his impressions and the sort of literature which he wished to write, which would certainly never have been of the "best seller" description, but I believe that the name of Andre Beaunier will go down the centuries as one of the most exquisite writers of his time. On two occasions Andre Beaunier showed great emotion. One was on the death of Oscar Wilde. He came to me white and trembling in a terrible state of depression. I had read and heard vaguely about Oscar Wilde but knew very little about him. I had read some of his poems and loved them and Andre told me something of his story, but when I questioned him as to the reason why Oscar Wilde was imprisoned, he blushed to the roots of his hair and refused to answer.

He held my hands and just trembled. He stayed with me very late and kept on saying, "You are my only confidante", and he left me under the strange impression that some uncanny calamity had befallen the world. Again shortly after, he appeared one morning with a white tragic countenance. He would not confide to me what was the reason of his emotion, but remained silent with set face and eyes staring before him and on leaving kissed me on the forehead in such a significant manner that I had a premonition that he was going to his death and remained in painful anxiety until—three days later—he returned in brilliant spirits and confessed he had fought a duel and wounded his adversary. I never knew for what reason the duel took place. In fact I knew nothing of his personal life. He generally appeared at five or six each afternoon and then he read to me or took me for walks according to the weather or our mood. Once we sat at the opening where four roads cross in the Bois de Meudon. He named the right-hand, Fortune, the left Peace...and the road straight ahead Immortality and "Where we are sitting?" I asked. "Love" he replied in a low voice—"Then I prefer to remain here." I exclaimed delighted—but he only said: "We can't remain here." and rose and walked very fast down the road straight ahead.

Very disappointed and puzzled I trotted after him calling out: "But why, but why, why do you leave me?" But he didn't speak again all the way home and left me abruptly at the door of my studio.

This quaint and passionate friendship had lasted over a year when in the innocence of my heart I had dreamt to give it another expression. One evening I plotted to send Mother and Raymond to the Opera and so be alone—that afternoon I clandestinely bought a bottle of champagne. That evening, I set a little table with flowers, champagne, two glasses—and I donned a transparent tunic and wreathed my hair with roses and thus awaited Andre, feeling just like Thais. He arrived, seemed very astonished and terribly embarrassed—he would hardly touch the champagne. I danced for him, but he seemed distrait and finally left abruptly saying he had a great deal of writing to finish that evening. I was left alone with the roses and the champagne and I wept bitterly.

When you recollect that at that time I was young and remarkably pretty, it's difficult to find an explanation of this episode and indeed I have never found one—but then I could only think in despair: "He doesn't love me". And as a result of hurt vanity and pique, I began a violent flirtation with one of the others of my trio of admirers who was tall and blond and handsome and as enterprising as Andre was backwards in embraces and kisses. But this experiment also ended badly, for one night after a real champagne dinner in a Cabinet particulier he took me to a hotel room booked as Mr. and Mrs. X. I was trembling but happy. At last I would know what love was. I found myself in his arms, submerged in a storm of caresses, by heart pounding, every nerve bathed in pleasure, my whole being flooded in ecstatic joy—I am at last awakening to life. I exulted—when suddenly he started up and falling on his knees beside the bed in undescribable emotion cried: "Oh—why didn't you tell me? What a crime I was about to commit—No, no you must remain pure. Dress, dress at once!"

And, deaf to my laments, he put my coat around me and hurried me to a cab—and all the way home swore at himself if such a savage manner that I was very frightened.

What crime, I asked myself, was he about to commit? I felt dizzy, ill and upset, again left at my studio door in a state of great discouragement. My young blond friend never returned; he left shortly after for the Colonies and when I met him years later, he asked: "Have you ever forgiven me?" "But, for what—?" I questioned...

Such were my first youthful adventures at the borders of the strange land of Love, which I longed to enter and which was denied to me for many years by this too religious and awe-inspiring effect which I produced upon my lovers—but this last shock had a decided effect upon my emotional nature, turning all its force toward my Art which gave me the joys which Love withheld."

BRICKTOP

Regine, who first owned nightclubs in France then internationally, is probably the only woman who followed in Bricktop's footsteps as a nightclub owner and performer of world reknown. Bricktop features in many biographies of British and American celebrities. It is said that the Duke of Windsor learnt how to charleston in her club in Paris and that if she didn't recognize you when you came through the door then you were really only "Nescafé" Society, a name coined by Noël Coward when in Paris. Here is a report from Bricktop herself about those days:

> "Paris in the twenties was the artistic capital of the world. I was in Harlem in the 1920s, I saw the excitement of the Renaissance there, but Paris was even more exciting. The whole city was like a great big ongoing celebration. World War I had been all too real to the French. Now that it was over, they wanted to forget all that heartache. They wanted to party and dance. The city was like a magnet to goodtime-loving people from all over the world.

> A lot of these people were rich Americans. They knew how to get the most value out of their dollar, which is why they were rich in the first place. In

Paris after the war the dollar was the best kind of money to have. My hundred-dollar-a-week salary at Le Grand Duc translated into something like two-thousand francs. Just a few years earlier it would have been only about five-hundred francs. And I was just a poor working girl. Imagine what the French inflation did for an American millionaire.

The nice thing about a lot of these American millionaires was that they didn't just bring over their money. They also brought over their interest in helping young writers and artists. Fannie Ward helped a lot of young people. So did Robert McAlmon and, later, Peggy Guggenheim.

There were a lot of young talented people around to be helped. Paris was filled with so many young people who didn't have a dime. They all clung together at the Dome or the Select, the two big places in Montparnasse—on the sidewalk in the summer, indoors in the winter. We entertainers joined them when we were through work. A lot of people who had money were there, too. Fitzgerald later wrote that in those days in Paris it didn't matter if you were broke, because there was so much money all around you.

Of course, by that time Scott was already successful and had plenty of money. The way he threw it around, he was naturally the star of the Paris art scene. Money burned in his pocket. When he'd go out for an evening, he'd stuff his pockets with bills. It's lucky he lived in a time when mugging wasn't the night-time sport it is today. He would usually stay out partying until all that money was spent.

Scott and his wife, Zelda, were a beautiful, fun-loving couple. They came into Le Grand Duc one night in the fall of 1925 with Dwight Wiman and his wife, Steve. The Wimans were regulars at Le Grand Duc, friends of Fannie Ward. After that first night, so were Scott and Zelda.

Scott was almost thirty, but he acted like a big, overgrown kid. Their baby, Scottie, had been born, and I couldn't believe Zelda was a mother. She was a wisp of a girl, feather-slight, with lovely hair and very white skin. She was very outgoing, but next to Scott she seemed almost retiring. He was so mischievous, he'd take over the whole place.

It as impossible not to like him. He was a little boy in a man's body.

◆   ◆   ◆

Of course, when that kind of thing happened, I could always say, "You can't do that in here, because this is Bricktop's." Starting a fight at Bricktop's was like starting a fight in somebody's house.

Everybody has arguments, of course, and these people were no different. There were no permanent rifts. Somebody'd get drunk and say to somebody else, "I've wanted to tell you this for a long time—," but there were never any knockdown, drag-out fights. Those people were too close.

As I've said, everybody was fooling around with everyone else. There was homosexuality, but it was pretty discreet. Most of it was done outside the set. I'd have gay men come into the club and say, "Bricky, I don't want to see the little boy that I gave five hundred francs to last night in here tonight. I know where to find him. I might come in with my wife or somebody."

You know those little boys, they'll tell you right away quick:"What's the matter? You don't know me tonight? You knew me last night."

In later years gay and straight people mixed more—I noticed it especially when I returned to America—but back in Paris before the war that kind of stuff was kept pretty much separate. There was a place in Paris called Le Boeuf sur le Toit. The name means The Cow on the Roof, and it came from a popular Brazilian tune of the early Twenties. Darius Milhaud, one of the avant-garde composers of the period who were called "Les Six", based one of his pieces on that tune, and it became the name of the bar. In the early Twenties, when it was on the Rue Boissy d'Anglas, Le Boeuf was a center for French writers and artists—Jean Cocteau, Erik Satie, Rene Clair, and many others—but by the late Twenties most of that crowd had drifted away. In 1928 the owner, Louis Moyses, moved the place to Rue de Penthievre, and it became known as a gay hangout, but very elegant. One of Moyses's managers in the second place was named Jacobi, and he later went to the United States and opened up a place with Bobby Short.

I went to Le Boeuf sur le Toit sometimes. They were nice people, well-mannered people. It wasn't like some of those gay bars they have now. Other legends of course are Edith Piaf and her protégé Charles Aznavour. They both starred at the Olympia but cannot really be regarded as theatre people although they knew everybody. A life of a singer is usually different from an actor in the fact that actors are working at 8 p. m. every night whereas singers and night club owners don't really start work till much later. Anyone studying the night life of Paris in the 1920's and will come across the life and times of Bricktop. Josephine Baker was a friend and the new wave of black artists, singers and musicians who came to Paris was started by Baker and Bricktop."

MAURICE CHEVALIER

Present-day megastars owe their fame largely to television or to rock music; Chevalier was famous in the pre-TV era. How did it happen? Chevalier's widow, Yvonne Vallee, whom he divorced in 1932, was still bemused by her countrymen's short memories. "These days nobody realizes what a star he was," she said. "He was like a king. The huge crowds at railway stations, the crowds of people outside restaurants, wherever he went, nobody remembers that." There was a time, in the early thirties, when Chevalier was far, far better known in America than Herbert Hoover, who happened to be president at the time.

One of the extraordinary things about Chevalier was that he came to fame the hardest way, then lost almost everything, then clawed his way back to stardom not once but again and again. It happened in World War I, after his return to France in 1935, at the close of World War II (with the collaborationist smear threatening to put an end to his career for good), and again in the early fifties when absurdly, he was branded as pro=communist in McCarthyite America.

On stage and in films, Maurice Chevalier celebrated the glory of his birthplace—Paris, the dazzling, seductive, eternal but ever-youthful Paris—with far more genuine emotion than he ever bestowed on love or beautiful women.

At the height of Chevalier's fame, his lavish revues at the Casino de Paris ritualized this worship of place: they had titles like "Toujours Paris," "Encore Paris", "Paris qui Jazz," "Paris en L'Air," "PA-RI-KI-RI." In the public's mind, throughout the world, the town's glamour was inseparable from his own. He became, especially in American eyes, the Parisian par excellence. The late president Georges Pompidou told him once that he would have made a better envoy to the United States than any professional diplomat.

14

GERALD AND SARA MURPHY, HEMINGWAY, SCOTT FITZGERALDS

Gerald Murphy, son of Mark Cross—founder of the famous New York based leather goods store—and his elegant wife Sara, are often considered the Lost Generation's golden couple. Handsome, talented, and wealthy Americans, suffering from what they called "an absence of cultural stimulation in America", in 1922 Gerald and Sara uprooted from their home at 50 West 11th St. in New York, and crossed the Atlantic to take up painting and friendship and live with a distinctive domestic panache in Paris and the Riviera.

Far from the suffocating constraints of upper-class American society, the couple merged into a vibrant social circle that included some of the most legendary figures in the Lost Generation that dominated social and artistic life in post-war Paris, then in the grips of the modernist movement.

Gerald would become a serious modernist painter, Sara would seek to create art out of everyday life itself. Although Gerald's output as a painter was by no means prolific, he is nonetheless seen to be one of the most important American painters of the twentieth century. Their Paris home at 23 Quai des Grands Augustins (or 1 rue Git-le-Cœur) along the Left Bank of the Seine, was parked just around the corner from the home of the flamboyant & unusual Dolly Wilde, niece of Oscar Wilde and close friend of Natalie Barney's. On the Riviera, they stayed at a villa rented by Cole Porter, returning the next year to find Picasso and his family installed in the Hôtel du Cap at Cap d'Antibes.

Dabblers in the arts, their generous hospitality and flair for parties attracted kindred creative spirits, from Jean Cocteau to Cole Porter to Dorothy Parker, and they always placed value on good friendships above all else. Sara once told F. Scott Fitzgerald: "I don't think the world is a very nice place And all there seems to be left to do is to make the best of it while we are here, and be very grateful for ones friends because they are the best there is, and make up for many another thing that is lacking. " By virtue of their generous inheritances, both were able to pursue a life of leisure on both sides of the Atlantic, with a dash of philanthropy mixed in, evidenced by their bestowing financial gifts to impoverished artists.

In 1924, the Murphys formed a close friendship with the Fitzgeralds, who had travelled to France in the spring, seeking tranquility for his work, penning The Great Gatsby during the summer and fall in Valescure near St. Raphael. He would later cast the couple as the fictional characters Dick & Nicole Divers in Tender is the Night. "I hated the book when I first read it", Sara Murphy later said, rejecting categorically "any resemblance to ourselves or anyone we know—at any time." While the Divers characters exhibited the couple's glamour, the tragic Divers marriage was a more apt reflection of Fitzgerald's own marriage to his wife Zelda than of the Murphys.

But portrayals of the Murphys could also be found in the work of both John Dos Passos and Ernest Hemingway—who they befriended and introduced to a woman Ernest later blamed for the demise of his marriage to his first wife, Hadley. His posthumous memoir of 1920s Paris, A Moveable Feast, he depicts an unnamed "rich" who seduced him into superficiality and infidelity, a portrait that bears all the earmarks of the couple.

Theirs was a marriage punctuated by drama and disloyalty, to be sure—Sara had close relationships with at least three other men Fitzgerald, Hemingway, and Pablo Picasso (who painted her portrait on several occasions), yet their union nonetheless endured over five decades. The real foundation of their happiness, they once said, were their children. It was this family stability which put them in a different league than the younger league of expatriate bohemians frequenting the cafés of Montparnasse. Instead, they formed friendships with married couples with children, couples who had likewise emigrated from America out of a sense of deep dissatisfaction.

"Of all of us over there in the twenties, Gerald and Sara sometimes seemed to be the only real expatriates." Archibald MacLeish once wrote. "They couldn't stand the people in their social sphere at home, whom they considered stuffy and dull.

They had enormous contempt for American schools and colleges and used to say that Honoria must never, never marry a boy who had gone to Yale. And yet, at the same time, they both seemed to treasure a sort of Whitmanesque belief in the pure native spirit of America, in the possibility of an American art and music and literature."

This belief in the American spirit infused their day-to-day life in Paris, where Gerald Murphy made every effort to introduce the natives to everything from American jazz—Jimmy Durante's drummer agreed to ship them the latest new jazz recordings every month—as well as other artifacts from his homeland, from gadgetry and books. He wowed friends with his long-time collection of old Negro folk songs and spirituals, such as "Nobody Knows the Trouble I've Seen" and "Sometimes I Feel Like a Motherless Child", which he sang with his wife in two-part harmony—at one point for French composer and pianist Erik Satie, at Mrs. Winthrop Chanler's Paris home. After listening to Murphy accompany the vocals with a simple arrangement for piano, Satie leaned over to Chanler to say, "wonderful, but there should be no piano. Have them turn their backs and do it again." After a repeat a capella performance, Satie declared as he left, "Never sing them in any other way."

Brasserie Lipp exterior

Such an anecdote is emblematic of the creative electricity that came to define Paris of the 1920s, which in many ways came to represent the center of activity for a whole new cultural ethos. Gertrude Stein wrote that, in contrast to its British neighbour, "France could be civilized without having progress on her mind, she could believe in civilization in and for itself, and so she was the natural background for this period."

Foreigners were not overly romanticized by the French, just part and parcel of the ongoing postwar art movement. "Every day was different," Murphy said of the magical era. "There was a tension and an excitement in the air that was almost physical. Always a new exhibition, or a recital of the new music of Les Six, or a Dadaist manifestation, or a costume ball in Montparnasse, or a premiere of a new play or ballet, or one of Etienne de Beaumont's fantastic "Soirees de Paris" in Montmartre—and you'd go to each one and find everybody else there, too.

There was such a passionate interest in everything that was going on, and it seemed to engender activity." And the Murphys constituted an integral part of that activity, forming alliances with all manner of writers, poets, painters and the like.

But it was their reputation as legendary party givers that elevated them to the status of celebrities, and they would adopt a motto by the 17th century poet George Herbert, which later became the inspiration for Tender is the Night: "Living well is the best revenge," the title of Calvin Tomkins' 1971 biography of the couple.

It was their ebullient parties that really cemented their reputation. Archibald MacLeish once wrote, "There was a shrine to life wherever they were…a kind of revelation of inherent loveliness. "

Deux Magots restaurant exterior

One could only imagine the sumptuous array of culinary delights served up by the Murphys at their soirées. Perhaps new potatoes with butter and parsley and a green salad, which Archibald MacLeish had a great liking for; poached eggs on a bed of creamed corn, with sautéed tomatoes on the side, a favourite of John Dos Passos; caviar and champagne, in memory of Ernest Hemingway and Scott Fitzgerald; or perhaps just goat cheese and Provençal olives on a crusty baguette.

Perhaps their most celebrated soirée took place in the spring of 1923, on the occasion of the Diaghilev company's premiere of Les Noces, the ballet by Stravinsky. Three famous composers—Francis Poulenc, Georges Auric, and Vittorio Rieti—were assigned to perform three of the four piano parts on the stage with the dancers, with the fourth part performed by a friend of Sara's and Gerald's, Marcelle Meyer, who was recognized as the leading interpreter of the new music.

The rehearsals for the ballet were faithfully attended by the Murphys and some of their friends, including Dos Passos. Even the young Russian choreographer George Balanchine travelled from Moscow specifically to attend the premiere, as Stravinsky would later relate in his Memories and Commentaries.

The buzz surrounding the ballet led the Murphys to plan a celebration to commemorate its opening. "We decided to have a party for everyone directly connected to the ballet," he was quoted in Calvin Tomkins' book, "as well as for those friends of ours who were following its genesis. Our idea was to find a place worthy of the event. We first approached the manager of the Cirque Medrano, but he felt that our party would not be fitting for such an ancient institution. I remember him saying haughtily, 'Le Cirque Medrano n'est pas encore une colonie americaine. ' Our next thought was the restaurant on a large, transformed peniche, or barge, that was tied up in the Seine in front of the Chambre des Deputes and was used exclusively by the deputies themselves every day except Sunday. The management there was delighted with our idea and couldn't have been more cooperative."

Tomkins' account paints a tantalizing portrait of the festivities that took place the night of June 17, 1923—recounting how Stravinsky eccentrically arrived first so he could inspect the seating arrangements in the dining room, re-arranging place cards as necessary. Comparing the event to the famous "Banquet Rousseau," in 1908, where Picasso and friends paid tribute to Le Douanier Rousseau, Tomkins offers a guest list constituting what he calls "a kind of summit meeting of the modern movement in Paris", from Picasso to Jean Cocteau. Les Noces conductor Ernest Ansermet was present as was Diaghileva, along with a handful of ballerinas from the company and two male principals

The conversations over cocktails on the canopied upper deck of the peniche were likely as colourful and interesting as the champagne dinner that followed downstairs in the salle a manger. The long banquet table was broken up every few feet by strange little pyramids of childrens' toys—fire engines, cars, animals, dolls, clowns—that the Murphys had bought at the last minute at a bazaar in Montparnasse.

Picasso reportedly found this most amusing, gathering together some of the toys and forming an impromptu artwork, topped a fireman's ladder with a cow perched on it!

With Ansermet and Marcelle Meyer providing piano music at one end of the room, and ballerinas dancing at the other, Jean Cocteau finally recovered from an earlier bout of sea-sickness and came back on board, only to penetrate the barge-captain's cabin and put on his dress uniform, then sporting a lantern while sticking his head in at portholes to report to passengers that the barge was sinking. More theatrics erupted from Diaghilev's secretary Boris Kochno, who with Ansermet managed to dismantle the large laurel wreath from the ceiling, and Stravinsky, who ran across the room with it, jumping through the center. As Tomkins recounts, "No one really got drunk, no one went home much before dawn, and no one, in all probability, has ever forgotten the party."

15

NOËL COWARD IN PARIS

Noël Coward was 20, when, for his first trip abroad, he visited Paris in 1920. Having started his professional career in the theatre at the tender age of nine, when he played in The Goldfish, a Christmas pantomime, Noël Coward, in the early twenties, was not only a successful young actor, but also a playwright in the making. He had already written several plays among which, The Rat Trap and I'll Leave it to You, two comedies which were to be produced respectively in 1926 and 1920. Having nothing better to do until rehearsals began for the latter, Coward decided to go to Paris with a friend, Steward Forster.

On his very first visit to Paris, Noël Coward chose the exclusive district of the Opera area which was to remain his beloved Parisian haunt throughout his life. Noël's friend, Cole Lesley, in his biography, The Life of Noël Coward, stresses that "throughout the 1920s Noël had been to Paris whenever he could." The capital of France was for him, according to his own words, "the gayest of gay cities." When there, his favourite walk would lead him from the Ritz Hôtel, Place Vendôme, across the Rue de la Paix, to the terrace of the Café de la Paix, where he would have a drink while watching the "beautiful people" pass by. This frequent and much appreciated leisurely stroll inspired his famous song Parisian Pierrot interpreted by Gertrude Lawrence in his 1923 musical London Calling!

During all the "années folles", Noël Coward met most of the celebrities of the Paris theatrical world: among the friends he most regularly visited there were Sacha Guitry, the famous actor-playwright with whom he has so often been compared, and his delightful second wife, Yvonne Printemps, the celebrated actress-singer:

"If she was playing, he would go before anything else to see Yvonne Printemps in her last opérette: she was for me", Noël used to say, "the epitome of that so often misapplied word: *Star*. She was the true, authentic article from the top of her head to the soles of her feet. In addition to this indefinable but unmistakable quality, she had one of the most individual and lovely singing voices I have ever heard."

Enthralled by her unique voice as much as by the enchanting actress herself, Noël Coward wrote a "play with music", Conversation Piece, for Yvonne who achieved a triumph in London at His Majesty's Theatre (February 1934). She performed the role of Mélanie, and Noël Coward that of Paul, Duc de Chaucigny-Varennes. But Yvonne's lover, Pierre Fresnay, who was to become her second husband, soon took over Coward's part.

During the interwar period Noël was, thanks to his numerous famous French friends, a most brilliant star of Paris life, as he was in London.

A few weeks before the declaration of World War II, Noël had been approached by Sir Campbell Stuart, a director of The Times, who suggested he should take a job in the Intelligence Service. With the blessing of the Foreign Office and Winston Churchill's lukewarm approbation, Noël Coward agreed to run the British Enemy Propaganda Office in Paris. Thus on September 7th 1939, "crammed with secret and confusing information," he flew to Paris "with a parachute and a sort of inflatable belt for keeping (him) afloat in the Channel." He was also carrying "a brief-case containing "The Papers", most of which were marked "Secret". As usual, Noël Coward first stayed at the Ritz:

Noël Coward had been selected for this secret mission because he was fluent in French, he had often visited Paris where he had many contacts in political circles and the literary world, and above all because he "was revered and adored by the French nation." Thus it would be easy for him to liaise with two great French writers: Jean Giraudoux, the then Minister of Information and his "right hand", the equally famous André Maurois. Noël would dine with both of them, in Montparnasse bistrots with the former, and with the latter, considered as his "opposite number", in "his exquisite house" in Neuilly/Seine,

The first thing Noël Coward had to do was to rent an office, which he chose: Place de la Madeleine, a few yards from the Opéra. And thinking that his Ritz address might sound a little too frivolous, with the aid of an old friend, Madame Guinle, he found a flat in Place Vendôme just opposite his favourite hotel, in Van Cleef and Arpel's corner.

As part of his mission, Noël Coward went to the British Embassy to call on Sir Eric Phipps, whom he had known for several years. He gave him a letter from Sir Campbell Stuart. The envelope was marked "Secret and Confidential". Noël relates the meeting with his usual sense of humour:

"Sir Eric gave me a dry Martini and a very good dinner, during which he tried with wily diplomatic suavity to coax my secrets from me. I think he said 'What the hell are you up to?, ' but I may be misquoting him. At all events I was forced to admit that I hadn't the remotest idea."

The arrival of the German troops in the capital of France was to put an end to Noël's rather vague propaganda mission, and on the evening of April 18th 1940 he left Paris.

"The Gare de Lyon was dimly lit owing to the "blue-out", but apart from this the departure seemed to be much the same as usual. I leaned out of the window of my sleeper talking and laughing with my see-ers off as I had done so often in the past; the familiarity of the scene was intoxicating and nostalgic at the same time—. . The train began to move, they laughed and waved, and Paris slid away from me for five years."

Visits to Post-war Paris

A careful survey of the diaries Noël Coward kept from 1941 to 1969 reveals 17 entries written from Paris which correspond roughly to as many visits. In November 1944 he agreed to appear in Paris for E. N. S. A. He played at the Marigny Theatre on the Champs Elysées.

"To return to Paris after four years' humiliation was a curious and sad experience."

When normal life resumed after the war, his trips on the Golden Arrow became more frequent, his sojourns in the Place Vendôme of longer duration. "There was so much to be done," he used to say. He loved to meet Parisian celebrities and the "jet-setters" of the time, who were still called "café society". When in the 60s this "beau monde" lost most of its glamour and sophistication, Noël would give it the name of "Nescafé society". Noël was receiving invitations from Coco Chanel,

Schiaparelli, Elsa Maxwell, the Duke and Duchess of Windsor and entertaining them in his own apartment. Duff and Diana Cooper, Marlène Dietrich, Lilli Palmer, Claudette Colbert, Maurice Chevalier, Jean-Pierre Aumont, Danny Kaye, Cole Porter were among his regular guests.

The most noteworthy event in his life during that period was, his own performance in French of his play Present Laughter at the theatre Edouard VII. The comedy had been translated by the celebrated French playwright, André Roussin, under the title of Joyeux Chagrins (1948). Though he had a few good performances, according to Noël himself, the "play was a flop…The audience was bad, the theatre half empty…The Press have been cruel. The truth was that the French people didn't care for the play." In fact, after the horrors of World War II, drawing room comedies had come out of fashion, and it has always been difficult for the French public to understand British humour.

In 1950 Noël had to leave his Paris flat for ever, as it had come up for sale and currency regulations being still stringent after the war. It was not possible to take money out of Britain for such an expensive purchase. Cole Lesley's poignant narration of their last evening in Paris shows Noël's immense love for a city which had always given him so much happiness.

Noël continued to visit Paris, always staying at the Ritz hotel, thus remaining faithful to his beloved Place Vendôme. In the late 50s and early 60s, he came regularly "to have an orgy of theatre-going." He saw "magical Marie Belle and young Jeanne Moreau in La Bonne Soupe, Jean-Louis Barrault and Madeleine Reynaud in La Vie Parisienne, and enjoyed a joyful reunion supper with Yvonne and Pierre after he had seen them in Père."

The magnificent Louis XIV Place Vendôme, famous for its most fabulous jewellers (Cartier, Chaumet, Chopard, Van Cleef and Arpel, Mauboussin), with the Ritz Hôtel and then with his own flat, was indeed the centre of Noël Coward's world in Paris. Through the Rue de la Paix his Parisian paradise extended to the whole Opera district. On its way to the Place de la Madeleine, the nearby Boulevard de la Madeleine led to the enchanting tiny Place Edouard VII, a great favourite of all English people as it presents the only statue of a British sovereign in Paris. There, King Edward VII, on horse back, faces his own theatre with quiet majesty. Noël Coward's office was a few yards from the Rue Royale, where Maxim's, considered the best restaurant in Paris can be found. It was Noël's regular canteen where he adored having a meal with his friends. That's where France's greatest comic playwright, Georges Feydeau, set one of his masterpieces, La Dame de chez Maxim. The British embassy, in the Rue du Faubourg Saint-Honoré, where Noël was a privileged guest, was a very short walking distance away from The Place Vendôme, the Madeleine and the Opera.

After his meals at Maxim's, Noël Coward would cross La Place de la Concorde, reputedly the most beautiful square in the world, walk along the XVIIIth century Cours la Reine, and reach his two favourite avenues: l'Avenue Montaigne and l'Avenue George V with the famous George V hotel. These elegant thoroughfares are the frame for two of his greatest comedies: in acts II and III, Amanda's flat in Private Lives is situated in Avenue Montaigne, and in Design for Living, Leo "must be raving! The George V! Oh dear, Oh dear! Leo at the George V! It's a glorious picture. Marble bathrooms and private balconies! Leo in all that grandeur! It isn't possible."

In fact, Noël Coward's Paris was rather small, limited to the streets where luxury so visibly prevailed. However it sometimes extended to Neuilly, the most elegant suburb, and to the artists' districts of Montmartre and above all of Montparnasse, the haunt of the world's intelligentsia in the interwar period. Like James Joyce, Henri Miller, Ernest Hemingway, Picasso, Van Dongen, Foujita, Modigliani, Coward visited "Montparnasse, the navel of the world" and its celebrated cafés, Le Dôme, La Coupole, Le Select or La Rotonde. A little further down Boulevard du Montparnasse, he would also dine at Oscar Wilde"s favourite restaurant, La Closerie des Lilas, situated in a charming lilac garden.

Like all artists around the world in the interwar period, Noël Coward's motto was the song of the French West-Indian popular singer Joséphine Baker:

"J'ai deux amours, mon pays et Paris"
"I have two loves, my country and Paris."

—Hélène Catsiapis

16

SACHA GUITRY & YVONNE PRINTEMPS

Sacha Guitry (1885-1957)was an actor, playwright, film and theatre director, a producer and a brilliant raconteur. He was witty, charming and hedonistic. He has sometimes been called the Noel Coward of French theatre, in the fact that they both introduced light, witty plays to a serious theatre going audience. Both men were friendly competitors both changed places and worked in Paris and London successfully. However Guitry, unlike Coward, was married five times, one of his wives being the actress Yvonne Printemps and he wrote comedies about marriage, mistresses and divorce.

He wrote over one hundred plays and made thirty films, three of them classics of the French Cinema. His mentors were Sarah Bernhardt and Mirabeau. He wrote two plays for Madame Sarah. His father, Lucien Guitry was the leading actor in Paris for many years and only once in the last ten years of his life did he play in any other play that was not written by Sacha. Lucien built a home near the Eiffel Tower, and Sacha inherited it on his death.

It was a showplace, with a long sweeping staircase the centrepiece for the house. Sacha used to dress in some of his stage costumes, perhaps as Napolean or King Louis X1V and parade around the house while dictating a new play. After going to the theatre, giving a performance, having dinner, he would retire into his study and continue writing whatever play he was working on. He would sometimes wake his secretary at 3 am to take dictation handwriting. As soon as yellow legal sized paper with his large one play opened he would begin writing another.

Lucien Guitry was probably as celebrated an actor in his day as Sacha was to become, and had also a European reputation. In St. Petersburg, where Lucien acted for the Czar and the imperial court, Sacha was born in 1885. For the next five years on account of the demands of Lucien's career, Sacha spent six months of every year in France, the other in Russia. Lucien's wife got fed up with this annual exile and with Lucien's philandering and sued for divorce. While the divorce was still pending, Lucien kidnapped Sacha and took him to Russia where they spent the next eight months, Sacha was five years old. On their return to Paris, where by now Lucien's wife had been granted her divorce and custody of their children, Lucien resumed his theatrical career. Lucien's wife then embarked on working as an actress herself, taking the stage name of Pontry. She remarked often to Sacha how much he was beginning to resemble his father. Once he answered her with "Did you know him then?".

Lucien had actually abducted Renee de Pont-Jest when she was twenty, taken her to London where he was married to her at Saint Martin's in the Fields church, with Sarah Bernhardt as one of the witnesses. Sarah Bernhardt remained one of her life-long friends.

Sacha had of course to go to school, which he did starting at the age of six. He didn't like school, was a very poor student, a prankster, and managed to get thrown out of most of the twelve schools that he attended. However he manifested an early talent for drawing, painting and sculpture and was able to earn money from this work. In 1904, Lucien offered Sacha, then nineteen, a part in a play he was doing, but during the run of the play they had a serious quarrel after Lucien had fined Sacha for being late for a performance and for not being properly dressed up on stage. Sacha stormed out, and for the next fifteen years they never spoke to or saw each other.

Sacha then moved to a hotel (Hotel du Canada) where he shared a room with a stage-struck friend Rene Fouchois, and began to read and memorise the French classical literature that he had neglected during his fruitless school days. During a holiday in Normandy in the same year, he saw two plays which impressed him greatly, and motivated him to write his first play which a producer friend put on at the Theatre des Capucines, followed by a comedy "Nono" performed the following year, 1905, at the Theatre des Maturins with enormous success. His next play "Chez les Zoaques" had a good run also, after 84 performances the leading man had to drop out and Sacha took his place, for the first time acting in one of his own plays.

For the next few years he wrote one flop after another. However that didn't stop him from getting married to Charlotte Lyses in 1905 ; she was an actress in

Lucien's company, and had the additional advantege of having a private income on which they could (just) live. He had been called up to do a year of military service ; as a married man he did not have to live in barracks, so they moved into 8 rue d'Anjou, the house next door at number 10 was occupied by Jean Cocteau. Charlotte also had a country house in a small town in Normandy, where Sacha amused himself by staging a ceremony, during which he gave the mayor of the town a medal and ribbon inscribed "Pour le Merite Agricole", a non-existent honour. However the mayor, oddly enough, was able to have it recognised by the French government, with himself as it first recipient.

However Sacha continued to write flops for the next six years, and it was not until 1911 that he had two hits in a row, "Le Veilleur de Nuit' and "un Beau Mariage.

Each evening, before he would leave for the theatre, he would have the chauffeur fill the car with bottles of champagne, food, flowers and a large assortment of posssssions that he might need at the theatre, and then on the return the car would be filled again. His route was simple, from the house to the theatre he was playing in. He seldom dined out as he preferred to dine at home. When he went to say at his home on the Riviera he was often seen dining at the Hotel de Paris in Monaco or at the Casino.
His life, like Noel Coward's was full of colour, and elegance. But it was not without hardship.
During World War Two he helped numerous Jewish friends escape or stop them from being deported to concentration camps, because the German generals in Paris were fans of his. They liked his work and respected him. However after the war, he was accused of being a collaborator, and when the same friends didn't come to his aid, including Colette whose husband he saved from deportation, he was sent to jail for 60 days. The shock of the imprisonment and the disappointment with his friends affected him greatly. It was similar trauma as the one Ivor Novello experienced when he also was sent to jail. They were both matinee idols and this seemed almost an act of jealously on the part of the forces in society that condemmed them.

He was at the top of the theatrical and literary world from the belle epoque to his death in 1957.
Many books have been written about him, one of which is just about his life in the south of France "Sacha Guitry and Monaco". He was fascinated by gambling,

and the glamourous Casinos, and the clientele. His friends used to come and stay at the house in Cap D'Ail where he still wrote every day, plannning his next production.

Besides his work in Paris, he also worked in London. It is interesting to note that King George V1 was a great admirer and so enjoyed his witty repartee that the night he went to the theatre, he went backstage during both intermissions and had to be asked twice to return to his seat so the show could be continued.

When he and his father opened a season at the Edward V11 theatre in Paris in 1920 the agent for the theatre was C. B. Cochran, the well known London impressario. He invited them both to London and booked them into the Aldwych Theatre. The season was a huge success. The actor Forbes-Robertson reported "I have never known a greater night in a playhouse", Seymour Hicks reportedly said to Gerald du Maurier... "I shall be ashamed to act again!"

Having a father who was so famous and well known in France must have helped Sacha become known, however it was his own talent that made him an even greater name than his father and it is Sacha who is still remembered in Paris. Unfortunately after his death, his house remained empty and unkempt, so it was sold to a real estate developer, and the bulldozers moved in. The sweeping staircase was exposed as the front walls came down, the upstairs hall of mirrors where they had kept original masterpieces of art, stood alone, until finally it all crashed to the ground.

Sacha had originally decided to give the house to the Academie Goncourt, who had honoured him years earlier, as a meeting place which they never had, but after the way he was treated in 1944 he decided against it. It was unfortunate decision. The house was unique and full of interest. It could have become a memorial to him and all the treasures he had, costumes, a huge collection of rare autographs, historic letters, his collection of art, and his own sculptures he managed to do in his spare time.

His funeral was held in the Montmartre cemetary where he was buried in the same grave as his father. It is said that eleven thousand mourners passed the coffin before the ceremony. The people who owed him so much during and after the war now came forth and told their stories, but it was too late for Sacha. His name, like Noel Coward's will always summon up a vision of a witty urbane superstar who knew how to entertain by writing sophisticated comedies and living the life of a successful theatre legend.

YVONNE PRINTEMPS

Even though there are still many photographs and reviews of her, and her roles, it again is very interesting to try and compare Yvonne Printemps with someone in the contemporary theatre. She was unique of course, and very French, her use of English was extremely limited with a pronounced accent. Perhaps a cross between a French actress today who stars in musical comedy and is also a celebrated society hostess. Is that possible in today's world?

She was born in 1894 to a poor family in a town just outside Paris. By the age of thirteen she was already appearing as a dancer at the Folies Bergeres and had been named Printemps (springtime) by fellow dancers because of her sunny disposition. Before her 20th birthday she was singing in a revue starring Maurice Chevalier and Mistinguett. She went on to study singing with the highly acclaimed vocal coach Mme. Paravini.

She became the second wife of Sacha Guitry with Sarah Bernhardt as a witness to the ceremony. Guitry wrote a huge amount of material for her and they played toegther in more than thirty of his productions before the break-up of the marriage in 1933. In 1923 she appeared with Guitry in his musical play L'Amour Maque which was an enormous success and in 1926 they went to London and played in Guitry's play "Mozart". Printemps wore breeches for this trouser part in which she portrayed Mozart as a youth.
The eminent critis James Agate wrote

> '*It is not exaggerating to say that on Monday evening people were observed to cry, and by that I mean shed tears, when Music's heavenly child appeared at the top of the stairs. At that moment of her entrance this exquisite artist made conquest of the house, and subsequently held it in thrall until the final curtain.* '

In 1926 they took Mozart to New York and later to Boston and Montreal. It was their first visit to America and she loved it.

In 1934 Noel Coward wrote the role of Melanie in 'Conversation Piece" for her and starred in the London production with her. Printemps spoke no English and had to learn her part phonetically. Her singing of 'I'll Follow My Secret Heart" was the highlight of the show.

An individually styled actress and vocalist, Yvonne Printemps made herself a star on every kind of stage. She left Guitry for the actor Pierre Fresnais and although they never married and stayed with him till his death in 1975. They were co-directors of the Theatre de la Michodiere in Paris and they starred together in many productions. Yvonne Printemps died in Neuilly on January 19, 1977.

17

EDITH WHARTON, OSCAR WILDE, NANCY MITFORD

EDITH WHARTON

It is difficult to compare any woman like Edith Wharton with a woman of today. Not only was she a wealthy beautiful socialite but she was a best selling author as well. It seems she lived in a now lost era...wealth, privilege, success as a writer and hundreds of admirers. She made over $20,000 for her novel The House of Mirth which would be the equivalent of $200,000 today. She had great houses in New York City and Newport, Rhode Island. She held great parties and knew the social set of each city.

Today we have wealthy fashion conscious socialites and we have famous best selling novelists but not a combination of the two. Great wealth, similar to the Rothschilds or the Vanderbilts brought recognition and acceptance in many circles, just as today...having the right connections are of supreme importance. However she loved Europe and had spent some years there in her childhood which she never forgot. In 1906, at the age of 44 she moved to Paris. Edith did not go to University, nor was she sent away to school, so she did not have access to the old boy network which is often the way to success today. Her father had a great library and she almost self taught herself, reading Russian, French and Italian history and art as well as languages.

In Paris, she rented George Vanderbilt's apartment on the Left Bank on rue de Varenne...a street with many mansions, hidden behind stone walls and great doors. Here she proceeded to entertain and become one of the top hostesses of Paris. Not only the crème de la crème of the Paris salons, but British and American visitors arrived, including the writer, Henry James who became a close friend.

Having money helped of course but to combine this social life of receptions. luncheons, teas and dinners with being a serious writer only proved what a truly remarkable and gifted woman she must have been.

It may be easier to achieve fame when one is rich obviously not only for the social connections but professional ones as well—publishers, lawyers etc. , —but Edith Wharton worked tirelessly: she wrote novels, travel books, diaries, an autobiography, hundreds of letters, as well as welcoming house guests and visitors to her home But who could do that today?

That era has gone, but if you walk down the rue de Varenne you can still get the feeling of what that world was like. Behind the great doors of these mansions are courtyards and gardens where the staff have separate apartments and the main house looks out on to the garden. In later years Edith moved to the country and had two houses with magnificent gardens with a team of gardeners to tend them.

Henry James was a close friend and often stayed with her in Paris. They criticized each others work and in her autobiography, Wharton tells of an incident that may have made James jealous. She had written an article in French and when James found out about it he swung around in his chair and said slowly.

"I do congratulate you my dear, on the way in which you have picked up every old worn-out literary phrase that's been lying about the streets of Paris for the last twenty years, and managed to pack them all into those few pages"...She writes "To this withering comment, in talking over the story afterwards with one of my friends, he added more seriously, and with singular good sense 'A very creditable episode in her career. But she must never do it again. ' He knew I enjoyed our literary rough and tumbles and no doubt for that reason scrupled the less to hit straight from the shoulder."

She adds that she was interested in James' technical theories and experiences but thought that he tended to sacrifice to them that spontaneity which is the life of fiction. They read each other's work, they motored nearly everyday in and around Paris especially in the heat, they lunched and dined together.

They would have dined at Le Grand Véfour, The Tour D'Argent, the Pre Catalan in the Bois, also many of the country inns outside Paris such as found in the village of Barbizon. Both of them loved Paris and most of their friends in later life were Europeans. Wharton returned to the States only once after settling in France and she died there at her country estate.

It would be interesting to know what she would have thought had she known that at least two of her novels would be made into very successful films...and how her novels would reach millions of more readers through these films, The House of Mirth and The Age of Innocence being made in the 1990's—almost 100 years after the books were first written. They brilliantly recorded the kind of life and times she had lived in New York, showing the wealthy, the socialites, the massive town and country houses they lived in, as well as the boredom and often insincere friends she wrote about. Her heroines were ideal roles for actresses, the settings were luxurious, her plots were fascinating and I'm sure it would have caused her great amusement to know about this posthumous recognition.

In her biography, she lists some of her close friends in Paris, and also when she lived and entertained in Newport. When she rented the Vanderbilt's apartment in the Rue de Varenne in the winter of 1906-07, it marked the transition to becoming a more or lest permanent resident of Paris, with Parisian friends, social acquaintances, jaunts into the surrounding countryside and establishing of writing. Her friendship with Morton Fullerton began, and developed into a passionate affair a little over a year later when her husband Teddy returned to America in March 1908.

Henry James accompanied her on a trip to Beauvais in May 1908, shortly before she had to return to America. He became her confidant and knew of her affair with Fullerton which continued until 1910. The French writer Paul Bourget, who had visited her at her house in Newport, Land's End, which she had bought in 1892, introduced her to his French friends including the painter Jacques-Emile Blanche and the critic Charles du Bos who later translated her "House of Mirth". Blanche's friends included Diaghilev, Cocteau, the Guitrys, Andre Gide, and the painter Walter Sickert. Edith met and became friendly with a notable Parisian hostess, the Comtesse Rosa de St. James, and attended her weekly salons. Edith was familiar with most of the writers both American and French who lived in Paris in the years before W. W. 1. She entertained the ex-President Theodore Roosevelt in 1910 year after he had left the White House and had finished a European tour, following which he asked the American ambassador to France to arrange a meeting with her. She asked him to tea.

She wrote constantly, and many of her novels were set in Paris. She sold her home "The Mount" in 1912. Her separation from her husband Teddy ended in divorce the following year. Her affair with Fullerton was over, and with her marriage also at an end she became close to Bernard Berenson and his wife—she had met him a few years earlier. She and Berenson went on a tour of Germany together; Berenson's wife chose not to go with them. Apparently Wharton was a very irritating travelling companion, very demanding and self-centered. However Berenson seems to have tolerated her behaviour and they remained life-long friends. She died at her country home in France in 1937

OSCAR WILDE

It is well known that after Wilde left prison in England he went to live in France (see the Barbara Belford biography of him, page 298). On February 13, 1898, he settled into the Hôtel de Nice at 4 rue des Beaux Arts. The same day Americans read about Reading Gaol in the daily newspaper as that was the day his poem The Ballad of Reading Gaol was published. In England everybody knew the author's identity, paying to read about his suffering. One shop sold 50 copies on the morning of publication.

Within a month, he experienced the tragedy of his wife, Constance's sudden death at the age of forty, in Geneva. She had had an operation to try to stop the terrible backache she had, but did not recover from it.

His book became a best seller and now that his wife was dead, and he was abroad with no family. It ended his artistic life and he began to live an existence as an overt homosexual.

"I'm so alone these days he said to the writer Gide. "I have lost the mainspring of my life and art, it is dreadful," Wilde wrote to Frank Harris. "I have pleasures, and passions, but the joy of life is gone. I am going under: The morgue yawns for me. I go and look at my zinc-bed there. After all I had a wonderful life, which is, I fear, over."

He knew he would never see his children again and there was no one left to outrage except himself and a few old friends. Will Rothenstein took him to dinner at an outdoor restaurant that featured an orchestra and Wilde tried to pick up one member of the orchestra, which was highly embarrassing to Will and he dropped Wilde after that. When they passed in the street Will cut him dead.

Twenty years earlier, he had never scribbled at the table at Brasserie Lipp or Deux Magots. He wrote letters instead. "I go to cafes like Pousset."

NANCY MITFORD

Nancy Mitford, one of the celebrated Mitford girls, author of the novel "The Pursuit of Love", became famous for inventing the British phrases "U" and non-U" describing people or behaviour, which are still used today especially in Europe.

Most of Nancy's books were best-sellers. She went to live in Paris after falling in love with a Frenchman, Gaston Palewski. Laura Thompson writes in her biography of Nancy: "And who knows? Maybe that was why she loved him so much; because in Gaston Palewski she saw another world and through him she glimpsed the possibility of escape to a place that would allow her to flourish as never before. Nancy was as English as tea and walnut cake at Gunter's, but it was only in France that this Englishness would truly bloom. More than almost anyone, she was an example of the freedom that moving to a foreign country can bring: the freedom to be her best possible self.

As a girl she had fallen for Paris—she had stood at the top of the Avenue Henri-Martin and felt tears gather in her eyes at its sheer sweeping perfection—and now, through her dealings with the Free French officers (not just Palewski), she had come to feel that this was the place in which she would be happiest, as liberated as France itself. "Oh to live in Paris, I'd give anything", she wrote to her mother in September 1944. Just as when she married Peter, back in 1933, she was in real need of a new life. Her old one held almost nothing for her.

She lived in various hotels, the Hôtel Pont Royal on the Left Bank shortly before she moved into her own apartment on the Rue Monsieur. The hotel is known as a "literaire" hotel, and many writers have lived there.

Her closest friends were Evelyn Waugh, Cyril Connolly; Cyril sent her "The Unquiet Grave" in 1944 and shortly afterwards she received a handsome copy of "Brideshead Revisited". This may have made her determined to start a book of her own.

Thus she began an illustrious career in Paris. She translated a play by the French writer Rosseau "The Little Hut" but as he understood no English she added her own jokes and dialogue without changing the plot of the play at all.

It was a huge success in England. She toured with theatrical company trying out the play in English provinces before its first night but was appalled by the carry-ings-on of the actors. Indeed she retained a horror of actors as a breed—"Unbri-dled by one ray of intelligence" she wrote and believed it all her life—although she took greatly to Robert Morley who played the lead who was a "normal, robust, bon-vivant kind of man and the only actor I've ever met who was a human being." Nancy phoned him to invite him for dinner at their hotel the next evening; "come at 8 o'clock", she said, "sharp". Morley had to explain that he would be doing the play.

"Do you do the play twice every night?" she asked, her head two centuries away at the Versailles theatricals run by Madame de Pompadour, usually for evening only.

Later in life she bought a house in Versailles and moved from the Rue Monsieur. Her lover married another woman; Nancy died of cancer aged 69, after a long and painful illness. The Mitford sisters, Jessica, Pamela, Diane, Unity and Debo-rah were all in the limelight during their life-times.

18

THEATRICAL RESTAURANTS OF PARIS

The two restaurants that claim to be the oldest establishments in Paris(although both proprietors will probably claim the title if you ask them) have theatre associations. These restaurants have been written up in history guides, their clientele includes Sarah Bernhardt, actors, playwrights and many others from the Comédie-Française and other nearby theatres.

The first is Le Procope, 13 rue de l'Ancienne Comédie in the 6th Arr. (The Comédie-Française was once situated across the street). It was originally a private house, the dining rooms are divided up into small rooms, on each level. When I was there last the new owners had tried to make it a kind of boutique restaurant with huge bowls of flowers everywhere which made the rooms seem even smaller. However if you want to dine where Voltaire, Jefferson and Benjamin Franklin used to dine frequently you will experience the historic feel to the place.

Bofingers restaurant, the oldest Brasserie in Paris

The second restaurant also claiming to be the oldest is Bofingers at 5 rue de la Bastille, across the river on the right bank, near the new Opera House. Old time waiters deliver huge platters of shellfish around the room over the heads of the clients, the art nouveau décor a feast for the eyes. Ismail Merchant of the Merchant and Ivory Film Company loved to eat here and thought of featuring it in one of his films. His book "Filming and Feasting in Paris" is a wonderful guide to his favourite places, which he sometimes included in his films.

Fouquet's restaurant, Champs-Elysées

Theatre related restaurants include Le Grand Véfour (see chapter), the elegant Train Bleu, located inside the Gare de Lyon, but the most famous theatre restaurant of today must be Le Fouquet, 99 Avenue des Champs-Elysees. Although it is regarded as a tourist trap by many because of its location on the Champs d'Elysees near the Etoile, it still caters to the theatre world of Paris. The two main awards in theatrical Paris…are the "Molières" the award being the equivalent of the Tonys in the USA or the Olivier Award in London, and the "Caesars" the Academy Awards of France. The after awards ceremony awards are often held at Le Fouquet upstairs in the banquet rooms. Here the crème de la crème of the acting profession celebrate not only French stars but any Hollywood or British stars who are in Paris at the time. The restaurant has been featured in many star's biographies as to be seen dining here in the old days was the height of sophistication and glamour. The glamorous all came here, thespians as well as people like Chanel, Colette, Coward, famous dress designers and their models. Alfred Hitchcock, Grace Kelly and many others.

The same applies at the Café de la Paix, 12 Boulevard des Capucines, near to the Opera House. It is a landmark and as many Gourmet guides such as Zagats say it is a "must" for old times sake. Go through the inside rooms to see the décor before sitting outside to"people watch" perhaps on a soft summer evening. Nearly always crowded it is said that if you sit there long enough you will see the whole world pass by.

Interior of Le Train Bleu restaurant, Gare de Lyon

There is something about a restaurant within a train station which is very theatrical. You only have to think of Noël Coward's "Brief Encounter' or "Anna Karenina" by Tolstoy to remember the emotion in those scenes. Train stations can signify all kinds of emotions within the human spirit. Just as arrivals and departures take place on stage there is the same kind of excitement at a railway station. The anticipation before the curtain goes up compares with an expected arrival then there is the curtain call. . the departure—as on a stage. The departure or arrival of a troop train, for example, can say it all, as far as human emotion is concerned. For many actors, train stations are short but important scenes in their lives. Most actors have stories of their touring days and meeting fellow actors at railway stations—Crewe station being the most famous one in England. Le Train

Bleu is not only one of the most beautiful, second empire dining rooms in Paris but its list of celebrities past and present is formidable. From Sarah Bernhardt to Colette, Cocteau, both Lucien and Sacha Guitry, Coco Chanel, Edmund Rostand and Jean Gabin.

Maggie Smith appears in a scene here from the film "Travels with My Aunt" from the book written by Graham Greene. Recounting her adventures when a young girl, as the "aunt' in a flashback to her youth. . she steals two champagne glasses hiding them in her fur muff, before running off with a stranger on the Orient Express which is departing on the tracks, just below her table in the Restaurant."It's all about glamour, romance and adventure." The train bleu was going to the Riviera and the south of France, conjuring up a wicked way of life and a sunny place full of shady people.

Terminus Nord 23 rue de Dunkerque, still on the right bank, has a magnificent 1920's interior, with great chandeliers, mirrors and marble all situated inside the Gare du Nord. It also has the aura of excitement and travel.

Another railway station restaurant which is historic with a Parisian decor is found in the Hôtel Concorde across the street from the Gare St Lazare, 108 rue St. Lazare. Monsieur Eiffel designed it in the same year that he built the Eiffel Tower. So you can imagine the creative and decorative room which is classical French and again has that aura of exciting travel about to happen, whether it be departures and arrivals.

The menu is classical also without the high prices of the most famous of them all. That would be either the Tour D'Argent, Maxims or the Ritz. These three restaurants have to be the most luxurious in Paris. If you can afford their astronomical high prices, and are on a business expense account then you can relax. However somehow even the view of the Notre Dame palls when you see the bill. The tables at Maxims are pushed together side by side, so that your neighbour beside you is sitting right next to you, and yet the French don't seem to mind this kind of trestle table seating.

The most fabulously expensive restaurant in the book is Le Grand Véfour because of its history and the list of clients, mostly writers, actors, playwrights and poets…within a stone's throw of the great Comédie-Française. (See Chapter Ten)

Many books have been written about the cafes where the "Lost Generation" of American expatriates, most of them writers and artists frequented on the left bank. Ernest Hemingway, Scott Fitzgerald, and many others immortalized these places. They each had their favourite café whether it be the Dome, or the Coupole or the Deux Magots, all very close to each other and serving the same kind of food. Hemingway's favourite The Closerie de Lilacs is further from the others, and there is a plaque in the bar in memory of him. The Brasserie Lipp is still regarded as an "in' place for book editors, writers and TV hosts, however to be seated upstairs is to be in "Siberia' and is unacceptable to these people. The food is mostly German, sauerkraut being very popular with German beer or their world renown sausages and mustard served on their own.

The waiters here can sometimes be surly and impatient so try to speak French to them. Jean Paul Sartre and Simon de Beauvoir ate there regularly then crossing the road to have the coffee in the Dome or the Select afterwards.

Isadora Duncan and her sister used to eat breakfast each morning at the Deux Magots...breakfast being the usual fare of a croissant and coffee. Imagine going to work on such a meagre meal but those were the days before Americans wanted something more substantial. It is curious to see in most cafes, on the bar or zinc counter, a stand or bowl of hardboiled eggs which the French eat at all times of the day except for breakfast...in fact, I think they don't appear on the counters till around midday. I often made a lunch of a hard boiled egg with a tartine du beurre at the counter...(a tartine being a split baguette(freshly baked) smeared with butter.)

It is interesting to note, that bakers are obliged by law to shape croissants made from margarine into a crescent while croissants made from pure butter must be straight.

When in Paris or if you watch French movies you can often see people eating a boiled egg at a bar...Yves Montand did it in several films including the romantic comedy, "Caesar and Rosalie" which also starred the late exquisitely beautiful actress Romy Schneider.

Obviously one wants to avoid tourist traps and the cafes that serve steak frites…a tiny thin steak with a huge portion of French fries…even if the fries are delicious, which they usually are, hence the name, it is not very satisfying.

If you do want to visit a well known restaurant without the crowds, go for an early lunch or dinner before the restaurants becomes crowded. In the Bois de Bolougne there is an elegant turn of the century place featured in many films, including Gigi called the Pre-Catalan. It is located in the park where the horse drawn carriages outside makes it look like the Tavern on the Green in Central Park. There are boats for hire nearby for rowing on the lake and on a summer's day the whole place looks like a Monet painting. The light, the shadows and the trees make it an ideal place for photographs as well. The restaurant is often closed for weddings and special events so it is wise to phone ahead for reservations.

Besides the view from the Tour D'Argent, the other memorable view is from the dining room named Jules Verne on the first floor of the Eiffel Tower. Named Jules Verne, the view is magnificent, stretching across the whole of Paris. Bookings are necessary but if you have to go to one tourist trap this should be the place.

Many visitors to Paris have never gone to the restaurant which is on the top floor of the department store on the Rue de Rivoli called the Samaritaine also has a wonderful view of the Seine and the surrounding area. Mostly for tired shoppers, often it is almost empty so it is nice to have a snack there at sunset and watch the ever changing sky.

19

JEAN COCTEAU, JEAN-LOUIS BARRAULT, PETER BROOK

JEAN COCTEAU

Cocteau was born in 1889 at Maisons-Lafitte, near Paris, into a comfortable, rich and well-connected family, and was described as an imaginative, clever, handsome and charming youngster. The family moved in 1899 to Paris, which became his favorite place. He said "I was born a Parisian, I speak Parisian, my accent is Parisian". In Paris he and his family lived with his grand-parents, at 45 rue La Bruyere. His mother attended the theatre regularly, and it was probably from her that he acquired his life-long interest in the theatre. He saw all the celebrated actors of his day, Rejane, Bernhardt, Mounet-Sully, the actress Colette, the "divine" Madame Barthet, Edouard de Max, as well as the music-hall stars, Yvette Guilbert, "la Belle Otero" and Mistinguett.

His father's death in 1899, when Jean was only ten, was a devastating blow to him; Cocteau was a poor student, lacking discipline. He began writing poetry at an early age, his first volume being published when he was sixteen. Edouard de Max, a leading actor at the Comédie-Française, arranged for a public reading of his poems at the Theatre Femina, and invited theatre celebrities as well as the most powerful critics, who praised Cocteau's poems in their reviews. Authors who attended included Rostand (Cyrano de Bergerac) and Marcel Proust.

He had achieved fame of a sort and in 1912 he moved away from home to take over a wing of the Hôtel Biron on the rue de Varenne. Another part of this mansion was occupied by the sculptor Auguste Rodin.

At this time, a stinging criticism of his poetry was published, and supported by Andre Gide. Cocteau realised that the criticism was justified, that the poems wee superficial, and lacked evidence of sincere feeling or of serious work. At that point he met Diaghilev, and through him Stravinsky, Poulenc, Ravel and other composers; he left Paris to live in his original home at Maisons-Lafitte, and then in Switzerland with the Stravinsky's.

When was broke out in 1914 he volunteered to join the French army but was refused on medical grounds; he tried to become an ambulance driver, was again dismissed. However during the war years he met Modigliani, Braque, but particularly Picasso, with whom he spent a great deal of time, as well as Apollinaire and other poets.

Cocteau was responsible for Diaghilev and Picasso meeting, and collaborated with them in the production of the Ballet Parade (1917), an aggressively modernistic work of art, which succeeded in scandalizing the theatre-going Parisians. The following year he published Le Coq et L'Arlequin attacking complicated music such as that by Wagner, Debussy and Stravinsky, which caused the last-named to be estranged for several years. In the early 1920s Cocteau devised a pantomime Le Boeuf sur le Toit, a play Les Maries de la Tour Eiffel, a novel Le Grand Êcart and a book of poems.

In 1923, after the death of his boy-friend Raymond Radiguet (author of Le Diable au Corps), he became so depressed that Diaghilev took him to Monte Carlo to recover.

There, however, he turned to opium; ultimately his family and friends persuaded him to go into a sanatorium where he remained for two months.

He then went to live in Villefranche at the Hôtel Welcome, where he wrote L'Ange Heurtebise, Oedipus Rex (with Stravinsky), Orpheus, Les Enfants Terribles, and Opium. He was one of the first to adapt or paraphrase classical Greek tragedies for the modern stage.

In 1930 he returned to a new apartment at 10 rue Vignon. He kept almost frenetically busy, he wrote plays (La Machine Infernale), poems, ballets, articles for Figaro, theatre criticism, a film, The Blood of a Poet. Through the thirties he wrote plays, and even during the Second War he continued to produce plays and films, designs, fabrics, frescoes, and 150 drawings for the decoration of a chapel at Frejus, which his adopted son carried out after his death.

In 1963, on October 11th, saddened by the death of his friend Edith Piaf, he died shortly afterwards.

JEAN-LOUIS BARRAULT

Jean-Louis Barrault was born in 1910 and died in 1994. In January 1931, when he was twenty, Barrault wrote to Charles Dullin, the director of the Atelier theatre and of its drama school, asking for an interview with him. Barrault was supporting himself at that time by working as a supervisor at the College Chaptal, where he was given board and lodging, but no salary.

Dullin realised that Barrault had no income but was determined to become an actor or at least to work in the theatre, so he offered to take Barrault on as a student without having to pay for his tuition at the Atelier theatre. This led to Barrault being fired from his job at the College Chaptal in July; Dullin then accepted him as a member of his troupe, to be paid 15 francs a day. On September 8th 1931, on his 21st birthday, Barrault began his stage career playing the part of one of Volpone's servants.

With his meagre salary Barrault was unable to pay his rent, so Dullin allowed him to sleep in the theatre. During the run of Volpone, the set included Volpone's bed, on which Barrault slept. His apprenticeship at the Atelier included learning make-up, and since the various minor roles he was given required making up for a variety of different characters, some of whom were so insignificant that they made only one or two appearances on stage, he nonetheless spent as much time, and took as much trouble as was needed for making up for these roles. He recalled in one production being the last in a procession of actors going on stage before the final curtain, and not being visible from any part of the auditorium as the curtain went down.

One of his tutors was the actor Decroux, who came to the Atelier from the Vieux-Colombier. Decroux taught Barrault the art of mime, spending weeks learning how to walk on stage, then later weeks learning how to mime riding a horse.

Before the 1934—35 season opened, Barrault had read a novel of William Faulkner's and wanted to mount a stage version of it. An inheritance on the death of his father allowed him to rent the Atelier from Dullin for a week at the end of the season. In due course the production opened, but was a total failure, only one critic writing a favorable review, the audiences laughing through or booing every performance.

Barrault spent from 1935 to 1937 principally making films. In 1937 Barrault returned to the theatre, for his first time as a director, of the Spanish play Numance at the Antoine theatre, also acting as producer. Other productions in other theatres, including the Atelier, followed. Having already done his year's military service in 1933, Barrault joined or was conscripted into the army again at the outbreak of World War Two.

In July of that year he was apparently in the unoccupied zone then controlled by the Vichy government, and was demobilised, played with the idea of forming a troupe of actors to play in Aix-en-Provence, but then settled in Toulouse. By pure chance he met there the treasurer of the Comédie-Française, who told him that Copeau, at that time director of the Comédie-Française, had been looking for him to play Rodrigue in the play Le Cid. Barrault immediately left Toulouse, was able to leave the unoccupied zone, arrived in Paris and signed up for his part on August 16th with Madeleine Renaud, whom he later married.

Barrault wrote in his memoirs about his feelings of reverence for the Comédie-Française, the ghosts of renowned actors who still seemed to inhabit the stage and the wings, the costumes, helmets worn by Edouard de Max, the cleanliness of everything, the polished floors, the innumerable activities of the back-stage staff. Soon after joining the company, he was present at the retirement party for a dresser, eighty-two old, who had worked there for sixty-two years.

Actors playing at the Comédie-Française fall into two distinct classes, "pension-naires" and "societaires". The first become members of the company for the duration of their engagement, year by year, and resign or are let go after giving or being given notice. The societaires are permanent members of the company, for life, cannot ever be dismissed or demoted. After twenty years they can only be made to retire, but even in retirement they are still members of the Comédie-Française, part of the management.

Barrault had started in 1940 at the Comédie as a pensionnaire. Two years later, he was offered the possibility of becoming a societaire. At about the same time, Jean-Paul Sartre suggested to Barrault to play in one of his plays "Les Mouches" at another theatre. Barrault was on the horns of a dilemma, on the one hand he wanted to do Sartre's play and not commit himself for life to the Comédie-Française, on the other hand both the status of being a societaire and the satisfaction at working in the most important and historic theatre in France were in his eyes extraordinary. After much hesitation he decided to refuse the invitation to join the Comédie and wrote a letter to that effect to the Doyen (Dean) of the Comédie-Française who presided over the relevant committee and delivered it in person. Having done that he went across the street with a friend to the café Univers for a drink. In a fit of panic he rushed out of the café, back into the Comédie-Française, and was able to send an official of the Comédie down to the committee room where his letter of refusal had been read, but luckily not yet acted upon, with his decision to accept the offer of societaire status, if it was not already too late.

It was not too late! With some misgivings he became a societaire in 1942.

In September 1945 while on a brief holiday in Normandy he was summoned to Paris by the government minister responsible for the Comédie-Française; the company was to go to Brussels to perform one of Paul Claudel's plays, "Le Soulier de Satin". The probable reason was to flatter Claudel who was at that point the French ambassador to Belgium. Barrault knew Claudel very well and they were good friends. The reunion with Claudel was very gratifying to both of them; the two scheduled performances took place as arranged, the reviews were ecstatic, and the company and Barrault returned to Paris quite elated.

Although the fact had never been publicised, over the course of the 20th century the Comédie-Française had become gradually but progressively under the control of the governments of the day. Although in theory the Comédie-Française was an independent, private theatre that could support itself financially, in reality it received financial support from the government with the condition that the traditional repertoire of classic French plays by the classic authors such as Molière be maintained.

When Barrault had joined the company he had been unaware of this, however in 1946 a commission of distinguished personages was appointed by the government to review the constitution of the Comédie-Française and to make whatever changes might be found appropriate. One of the recommendations was that the existing societaires would be asked to commit themselves to membership for life in the Comédie-Française. The point of all this is not obvious, since the actual changes in the constitution are not outlined in Barrault's book, but apparently many societaires took offense, as Barrault did, saying it was like a nun being asked to take the veil for the second time. He announced his intention of resigning and was relieved of his membership and of future participation in the Comédie-Française on September 1st 1946. Madeleine Renaud left some time later.

No longer being committed to the Comédie-Française, Barrault and Madeleine Renaud decided to found a theatre company of their own, and were joined by, among others, Pierre Brasseur, Edwige Feuillere. They were made welcome at the Theatre Marigny by the then director, Simone Volterra. Most of the plays performed were modern, and just like actors in Great Britain, were obliged to supplement the income from their theatre work by performing in films.

In his book "Memories for Tomorrow" he recounts the highlights of his career as well as the offstage struggles. He writes of hair-raising stories of missed planes, revolutions, broken limbs, no understudies, and to make a tour for the British Council seem like a charter holiday. His theatre, the Odeon was occupied by the student risings in 1968 just another day in the life of an actor whose work spanned 60 years in the theatre. He was a great inspiration not only to actors, but hundreds of French theatre goers who followed his career and that of his wife Madeliene Renaud. Just as the Oliviers were the theatre couple in London, producing their own productions, so too was the Renaud-Barrault company in Paris.

PETER BROOK AT THE THEATRE DES BOUFFES DU NORD

Peter Brook is one of the world's legendary theatre directors. His productions are a byword for imagination, energy, and innovation. From his ground-breaking production of Marat/Sade, to his "white-box" A Midsummer's Night's Dream, to his monumental staging of The Mahabharata and beyond, Brook has always been the pioneer of what a director and a company of actors can conjure out of an empty stage.

As a brilliant young man influenced by the theatrical visionary Gordon Craig, he turned his hand to Shakespeare, opera, new French drama, and mainstream comedy. Following Craig's philosophy, Brook began to search for a simplicity, harmony, and beauty that would incorporate all aspects of the stage production under the control of one person. He also began the lifelong search for authenticity on the stage, a search that led him around the world from London to New York, to his legendary Theatre des Bouffes du Nord in Paris, to Broadway and the Brooklyn Academy of Music. It was in Paris, in the 1970s, that he attempted to discover a universal language of theatre with an international group of actors. This collaboration resulted in a series of visually spectacular and innovative shows including The Ik, The Conference of the Birds, and The Mahabharata.

In his long and influential career, he worked with some of the world's greatest actors and writers including Glenda Jackson, Paul Scofield, John Gielgud, Laurence Olivier, Irene Worth, Jeanne Moreau, Peter Weiss, and Truman Capote. His films, such as Lord of the Flies, Moderato Cantabile, King Lear (with Paul Scofield), The Beggar's Opera, and the film of Marat/Sade moved the camera and the screen to borders they had not reached before. His book The Empty Space continues to be one of the classic works on theatre and drama in the Western canon and his memoir, Threads of Time, gave us a glimpse into his personal development.

Paul Scofield said that as an actor he had found Peter Brook to have an extraordinarily concentrated and penetrating understanding of the emotional and practical requirements demanded by the needs of authors and actors.

He had been a notably gifted and appreciated theatre director in London since the early 1950s, working also at Stratford and the Covent Garden Opera house.

During the rein of impresario Binkie Beaumont in London, Peter directed for "The Company of Four" production team which was modelled on Jacques Copeau's "Companie des Quinze" in Paris. Their aim was the produce plays which were more innovative then the West End could take. Brook also directed Jean-Paul Sartre's play, "No Exit' at the Arts Theatre which was a private club at that time. He went to Paris as often as he could for inspiration. He admired Jean Anouilh's plays, Jean-Louis Barrault's work and his production of Claudel's epic theatre. He admired Roland Petit's jazzy ballets and decided he wanted to work there.

His major move to Paris in 1970 was probably in large part a result of his feeling that theatre in England was suffering from its own success and from the pursuit of perfection, that it had become traditional and hide-bound. He had also embraced certain metaphysical ideas, notably those of a Russian philosopher Gurdjieff, and wanted to make contact with a leading scholar and exponent of Gurdjieff's teachings, Jeanne de Salzmann. His own notions of theatre included the surrealist movement

Brook was also a fluent French speaker, had produced plays in Paris, and had a French theatrical agent, Micheline Rozan. She was instrumental in finding space for him to start their Centre for Theatre Research, and for getting grants from American foundations, from UNESCO and David Merrick's foundation. Peter Brook assembled an international polyglot group of actors, and with their help the first production, with an invented artificial language, a surrealistic, symbolic, largely improvised piece came into being. Brook took this troupe of actors and the play to Persia, and after a long audience with the Shah of Persia's wife, the performance took place in the open air.

Another play, "The Conference of the Birds", equally surreal and somewhat metaphysical, was performed in Brooklyn and also made its way to California.

Meanwhile Micheline Rozan had found an extremely dilapidated empty theatre, called the Theatre des Bouffes du Nord, at the corner of the Boulevard de Roch-echouart and the Boulevard de la Chapelle. Brook decided to make it "home" for his troupe; he had been invited to direct a Shakespeare play for the Festival d'Automne in 1974, and put on "Timon of Athens" in a French translation by Carriere at the Bouffes du Nord. The play at the Bouffes was up-dated to take place in modern times, Timon becomes the C. E. O. of a large corporation, and the other characters similarly modified.

Another young British director Simon McBurney went to Paris. His theatré de Complicite has done a huge volume of innovative work in 21 years, going from comedy improvisations inspired by his mentor and teacher the French mime, Jacques Lecoq to Brecht, Durrenmatt and John Berger.

McBurney talks about the influence and importance that "Brook's Carpet" was to him, the practice of simply unrolling a carpet where you can create an acting space or stage, and now you can see this carpet in many Complicité shows.

In June 2002 David Hare attacked Brook and wrote that Brook had "drained plays of any specific meaning—an universal hippie babbling which represents nothing but fright of commitment." Brook was annoyed and hurt, the two began an interesting correspondence and no doubt have had many dinners together since.

In the meantime the Theatre des Bouffes du Nord was an inspiration to, not only British actors and writers but became famous world wide and attracted artists from across the globe.

20

SUMMING UP

In mid July 2005, it was announced that the Comédie-Française would be installing subtitles in English in the theatre for the very first time. This indeed may dismay some Frenchmen but will indeed please many English speaking visitors and no doubt will increase the audiences at the famous historic theatre. At last there will be a theatre troupe which British and American thespians can truly appreciate. It should revolutionize the Paris theatre scene. Many of the most brilliant actors work at this theatre but because they speak only French their names and reputations are not very well known outside France. Now all that should change. They may be still speaking French but at least you will be able to follow them in English and appreciate their talent.

In the past, only the actors who worked in French cinema were known overseas. Cocteau and Sacha Guitry made films years ago but their work never really became popular and it wasn't until after the war that French films got the distribution they badly needed abroad. The actors started to become known, especially when Bridgette Bardot came on the scene. , in 'God Created Woman" That film seemed to create a world wide interest in French films. Jeanne Moreau had already made 'Jules and Jim' which was considered an art film abroad. Then came Catherine Deneuve in Jaques Demy's 'Umbrellas of Cherbourg", and her international career was made. She is the daughter of veteran French actor, Maurice Dorleac and her mother was also an actress, Her elder sister, Francoise Dorleac was an actress but was killed in a tragic car accident early in her career.
Deneuve started as a model but was quickly discovered and cast in many films. She also was chosen as a model for the symbolic "Marianne" busts which are displayed across the country to represent France, this honour being held previously by Bridgette Bardot. She was formerly married to the British photographer David Bailey and has children by Roger Vadim and Marcello Mastroianni.

Although the actors in the legitimate theatre in Paris are well known in France it is the film stars who are known outside France, from Jean Gabin to Jeanne Moreau and Gerard Philippe, Catherine Deneuve and Gerard Depardieu. Their success has been helped obviously by subtitles. Now, as on Broadway and London, these film stars are returning to the stage in Paris, Philippe Noiret and Anouk Aimee playing in A. R. Gurney's 'Love Letters' for example.

The annual theatre and film awards don't get much publicity abroad, in comparison to the Oscars, the Oliviers, and the Tonys however these festive occasions do take place for the crème de la crème in Paris. . and the acting profession is there in full force.

Catherine Deneuve and Gerard Depardieu may not want to act in the legitimate theatre as their reputations were made in the film world. So it will be interesting to see if the stars of the Comédie-Française will now be known by an English speaking audience.

When Yves Montand made a film with Marilyn Monroe he suddenly became famous outside France, even though he had made 'Wages of Fear" many years earlier. Most people think of Yves Montand as typically French even though he was actually born in 1921 in Monsummano, a small town in Tuscany, where his father Giovanni Livi was a broom-maker. Yves baptismal name was Ivo. At the end of January 1924 the father Giovanni arranged with a smuggler to cross the mountains to Marseilles where he arrived on 2nd February; his house in Monsummano had been burnt down, apparently because he was a Communist. His family, including Ivo, followed in May 1924. Montand's entire childhood was spent in dire poverty. However in Marseilles he went to school, but left when he was eleven to work in a factory. The family needed the money. His sister Lydia set up shop as a hairdresser, employing her mother and, when he was thirteen, Ivo, who got professional training and earned a diploma in this profession. However he was not interested in the work, many of the clientele were prostitutes and he became familiar with many underworld figures. When he was seventeen, with the encouragement of friends he began to sing professionally in local halls and eventually in cinemas. However his real start came when he was hired to sing at the Alcazar, the vaudeville theatre where Maurice Chevalier had also started.

The Second World War in 1939 led to the collapse of France and the division of the country into the occupied zone and the "French State" controlled by Marshal

Petain; Montand, not able to make a living as a singer, took a job in a shipyard as a metal-worker, but the shipyard closed three months after he started. He got a job as a dockworker, always keeping practising his singing

However in 1941 he resumed his professional musical career at the Bompard cinema, then at various other music-halls in the region, his repertoire included many imitations of Charles Trenet, Fernandel and Chevalier. He got an agent, Audiffred, who obtained contracts for him in Lyon and Toulon as well as in the Marseilles region, and later around Provence and Nice. Montand had his eyes on a film career, and on January 21 1942 had a walk-on role in a film by Pagnol. But in March 1941 he was conscripted into one of the newly-founded work-camps where he had to stay until October 1941.

He returned home and was again taken on by Audiffred and again toured Provence, now earning a fairly good living. A new order by the Vichy government conscripting young men for work camps in Germany spared Montand only through the efforts of his sister Lydia and the help of a local fascist whom she approached. However the situation was still dangerous, but his agent made arrangements for Montand to get work in Paris where he arrived on February 17th 1944. He was to work at the ABC, a vaudeville theatre on the boulevard Poissoniere in Pigalle, where both Charles Trenet and Edith Piaf had already worked. He was an outstanding success and performed subsequently at the major music-halls, night-clubs and cabarets of Paris. Finally he met Edith Piaf who after some hesitation arranged for him to star with her on the stage of the Moulin Rouge. She fell in love with him, showered him with expensive gifts and had her song-writers write songs for him, and took him to appear with her on a tour of the South of France at the end of 1944. She met his family and became friendly with, in particular, his sister Lydia.

Back in Paris their love-affair continued, but Montand had become as big a star as Piaf, and professional rivalry led to jealous and quarrels. She did help him with his career, and arranged for him to get a part in a film "Les Portes de la Nuit" in 1946, a flop. He then returned to singing, got a part in another film "L'Idole" about a boxer, signed a film contract with Jack Warner apparently without reading it; later he got it translated into French and found it was a seven-year contract, standard but totally biased in favour of the studio. He refused to agree to it, the studio sued him, the lawsuit dragged on and was dropped when it became clear that Montand could not get a visa for the U. S. A. on account of being a communist.

In 1946 he starred in an operetta Le Chevalier Bayard, it was a critical and popular success initally but closed after a month because of poor attendances. He resumed his club and theatre performances and grew in fame and popularity while Piaf's star was setting. He was invited to sing at the wedding of Prince Aly Khan, (the son of the Aga Khan) and Rita Hayworth in 1949 at Vallauris near Cannes, and was flown down and back to Paris the same day, in order to fulfill his obligation to perform at a club in Paris that evening.

In August 1949 he met Simone Signoret, they were married in December 1951—her parents were Jewish. She had divorced her first husband, Yves Allegret. In 1952 Montand played the truck-driver in The Wages of Fear by Clouzot; it won awards at the Cannes Film Festival the following year. He then became known as a talented actor and a series of films started off his career. He suddenly became one of France's top actors. In the 80's he returned to singing and went to New York to give a concert from the stage of the Metropolitan Opera House at Lincoln Centre.

Although he lived mostly in Paris it is well known that he and his wife became partners in a restaurant in the south of France where they spent part of the year at St. Paul de Vence, a hill top village not far from Grasse. He relaxed there between making films and there are still photos of him for sale in the village, playing boules in the village square with the locals.
Maurice Chevalier achieved world fame, as an actor, when he acted with Leslie Caron in 'Gigi" and with Audrey Hepburn in 'Love in the Afternoon' even though he had had a long career as a singer and a music hall artist a long time earlier.

Paris has always been the most romantic location for a film, many American producers have made film there including Woody Allen and Billy Crystal. Elizabeth Taylor and Van Johnson starred in 'The Last Time I saw Paris" which had a great musical score and unforgettable lyrics that made the film so endearing to many Americans.

When Audrey Hepburn played the chauffeur's daughter in the film 'Sabrina" many American and British girls desperately wanted to go to Paris to try and achieve the transformation that she had obviously achieved, with or without Humphry Bogart.

When Elizabeth Taylor and Richard Burton's affair was in full swing, they stayed at the Hôtel Lancaster and according to Liz Smith who was with them often, all they could think about was food and where to eat in Paris.

When the stage play 'La Cage Aux Folles' first opened in Paris at the Palais Royal Theatre the two French actors who were well known stage actors, suddenly became known for their remarkable performances and went on to make the film, before the play was turned into a musical.

Michel Serrault became a film star and if you watch many French films, you will see him in dozens of interesting roles from years ago. Hopefully all these artists will still have the choice either to act on stage or in film; the problem has always been the language and the access to an English speaking audience.

Now, there has been a renewed interest in visiting Paris and especially the Louvre Museum. Since best selling book, The Da Vinci Code was published, there have been tours planned to view the sites mentioned in the book and a curious excitement about the fascination about a story which has historical and theatrical twist. No doubt the movie will increase this interest even more with Hollywood actors appearing in Paris and high-lighting the excitement of the theatrical scene.

The idea that people would visit the Louvre Museum for any other reason than to view the paintings seems ludicrous, but it appears that the first scene in Dan Brown's book is now gaining just as much as attention as the Mona Lisa.

Just as the city of Paris keeps being immortalized in movies such as "An American in Paris," "Gigi," "Love in the Afternoon", so again the world of entertainment has brought forward yet another reason to visit Paris. The Da Vinci Code and its setting may have started a whole new interest in the old buildings in Paris. Could we next have Murder at the Comédie-Française…or Missing in Montmartre? The search for theatrical events may become similar to the old days when Sarah Bernhardt had two hundred carriages ordered for her guests to ride from the Grand Hôtel to her theatre for her performance after a banquet. The younger generation who visit Paris may want to search out movie locations, just as I, when young, searched out Chopin's apartments in Paris after seeing the film 'Song to Remember' the story of Chopin's life.

Following the Da Vinci Code dramatic opening scenes either in the book or movie, and viewing the actual location where it happened, may be one way of enjoying a theatrical feast in Paris, with or without the Hollywood actors. I just hope that some of these visitors might search out the other fascinating and dramatic theatrical places of the past. It was in the Louvre after all, where Molière's plays were performed for the King and one wonders if they were played in the same spot as the opening scene of the Da Vinci Code.

The enjoyment of a good story or an exciting play which stimulates us and captures our imaginations remains: it is an added benefit to any visit, especially when it takes place in a glorious city such as Paris. It satisfies us in our endless quest for knowledge and leads us away from the obvious tourist attractions which any city serves up, leaving us with a fresh approach to seeing a city so rich in creative and theatrical history.

POETRY

The Wardrobe Mistress

Saddened by dreams of what she might have been,
Sick with the thoughts of what she is today,
She droops, a little woman, pinched and gray, Within the shadow of
    a painted scene;
Still lingers on her weary face the sheen
Of make-believe; the cruel crow's-feet stray
Beneath her faded eyes, and mute dismay
Lurks in her timid and pathetic mien.

Echoes of by-gone triumphs wake her breast—
The nights of tinselled bliss, the dizzy whirl,
The sparkling gauds, the limelight and the band—
Now with a needle in her work-worn hand,
She potters round the wings, all drably drest,
Stitching the trappings of some thoughtless girl.

                —John Ferguson (1912)

An Actor's Life

If I might choose my destiny
An Actor's lot be mine!
For half a dozen other lives
With his own life combine.

Tho' he's poor by fortune's malice,
And tho' his coat be bare and old,

Night bestows a regal palace,
And he'll robe, in cloth of gold!

Such is the players' magic story,
Passing quick from grave to gay,
Up and down,
Rags and crown,
Rich tomorrow poor today.

If larder lack, or cellar fail
What actor should repine?
He quaffs an empty cup
And on a wooden joint can dine!

Actors too can flourish after
The dagger sharp, the poison bowl!
Groaning's kill'd by sudden laughter
While a jolly song they'll troll!

Such is the player's magic story,
Passing quick from grave to gay, Up and down,
Rags and crown,
In the self-same day!

—H B Farnie (c. 1870)

ANECDOTES

If you are lucky enough to have lived in Paris as a young man, then wherever you go for the rest of your life, it stays with you, for Paris is a moveable feast.

—Ernest Hemingway to a friend in 1950

I was formed by the past, continued Labrousse. The Ballets Russes, the Vieux-Colombier, Picasso, Surrealism; I would be nothing without all that. And of course, I want to make an original contribution to the art of the future, but it has to be the future of that tradition. One can't work in a void; that leads nowhere.

—Simone de Beauvoir

Ionesco: (at a Left Bank café table, spying Beckett and Genet strolling past in animated conversation) *Hey! Sam! Jean!*

Genet: *Hey, it's Eugene! Hi there, Eugene boy.*

Ionescu: *Sit down, kids.*

Ionescu: (Rubbing his hands together) *Well, what's new in The Theatre of the Absurd?*

Beckett: *Oh, less than a lot of people think.* (They all laugh.)

—Edward Albee, "Which Theatre Is the Absurd One?"

Theatre people in Paris depend on cafes for sustenance, sometimes even artistic sustenance.

Cafés are important to actors, often dwelling far from their theatres, always working long and late hours while most of the world sleeps. Bar, bistro and brasserie are varieties of the ubiquitous café, and the café as stage set has entered 20th century drama, as the public square was often the setting for a classical French comedy.

Madame Patti was conducted by Jaques Offenbach when she sang in the Opera Salon at the Grand Hôtel.

Jean Anouilh, the French playwright wrote 21 full length plays during a span of 26 years.

George Sand has four plays running simultaneously in Paris.

Sarah Bernhardt said *'I have often been asked why I am so fond of playing male parts...As a matter of fact, it is not the male parts, but male brains that I prefer.*

—The Art of the Theatre, 1924

Jean Cocteau first production was a ballet plus mime by the Fratelli Brothers at Le Boeuf-sur-La Toit but speech was used in his "Les Maries de la Tour Eiffel"

J. G. Bennett, founder of the New York Herald Tribune sent Stanley off to search for Doctor Livingstone at the head of the Nile from the Grand Hôtel.

"There's something about Paris that always makes me feel fairly full of espieglerie and joie de vivre", Bertie Wooster once remarked.

"Why have I bothered to go through the marriage ceremony with each of my wives?I have done so, Madame, for the sake of my English public"

—Sacha Guitry

"To Sacha Guitry who, like myself, does not write in chains, and who, indeed, should have written this play."

—George Bernard Shaw (Inscribed on Sacha's copy of St. Joan.)

APPENDIX A

ROLL CALL

This is an incomplete list of actors from France, which generally means those who reside in France or those who have appeared largely in French film productions. The origin of this list is in collation of actor-stubs that contain reference to the actor or actress being an "French actor" or other indicative phrase. It also includes all actors in Category:French actors (as of 2005-03-24). Persons are listed alphabetically according to their surname.

Singly named persons

* Arletty
* Bourvil
* Capucine
* Coluche
* Fernandel
* Fréhel
* Miou-Miou
* Mistinguett
* Polaire
* Rachel
* Raimu

A

* Isabelle Adjani
* Renée Adorée
* Anouk Aimée
* Madame Albert
* Catherine Allégret
* André Antoine
* Fanny Ardant

* Yvan Attal
* Jeanne Aubert
* Stéphane Audran
* Claudine Auger
* Jean-Pierre Aumont
* Daniel Auteuil
* Charles Aznavour

B

* Josiane Balasko
* Nicolas Anselme Baptiste
* Brigitte Bardot
* Jean-Louis Barrault
* Marie-Christine Barrault
* Monica Bellucci
* Jean-Paul Belmondo
* Sarah Bernhardt
* Claude Berri
* Bertrand Tavernier
* Suzanne Bianchetti
* Juliette Binoche
* Carole Bouquet
* Charles Boyer
* Pierre Brice
* Emmanuelle Béart

C

* Jean Carmet
* Martine Carol
* Leslie Caron
* Vincent Cassel
* Laetitia Casta
* Daniel Ceccaldi
* Marie Champmeslé
* Maurice Chevalier
* Corinne Clery
* Aurore Clément
* Alice Cocéa

* Claudette Colbert
* Benoît-Constant Coquelin
* Ernest Alexandre Honoré Coquelin
* Clotilde Courau
* Valérie Crunchant

D

* Béatrice Dalle
* Marie-Louise Damien
* Lili Damita
* Danielle Darrieux
* Jamel Debbouze
* Virginie Déjazet
* Alain Delon
* Julie Delpy
* Catherine Deneuve
* Gérard Depardieu
* Patrick Dewaere
* Françoise Dorléac
* Jacques Dutronc

F

* Charles Nicolas Favart
* Frédéric Febvre
* Lolo Ferrari
* Edwige Feuillère
* Brigitte Fossey
* Pierre Fresnay
* Louis de Funès

G

* Jean Gabin
* Charlotte Gainsbourg
* Judith Godrèche
* François Jules Edmond Got
* Eva Green
* Juliette Gréco

* Georges Guibourg
* Lucien Germain Guitry
* Sacha Guitry

H

* Jane Hading
* Françoise Hardy
* Isabelle Huppert

I

* Eva Ionesco

J

* Irène Jacob
* Jacques Gamblin
* Claude Jade
* Marlène Jobert
* Louis Jourdan
* Louis Jouvet

K

* Valérie Kaprisky
* Tchéky Karyo
* Mathieu Kassovitz
* Salim Kéchiouche
* Véra Korène

L

* Dominique Laffin
* Karen Lancaume
* Samuel Le Bihan
* Jacques Lecoq
* Adrienne Lecouvreur
* Virginie Ledoyen
* Jean Lefebvre
* Max Linder
* Vincent Lindon

* Sylvia Lopez
* Aurélien Lugné-Poe
* Jean-Pierre Léaud

M

* Jean Marais
* Marcel Marceau
* Sophie Marceau
* Olivier Martinez
* Mathilda May
* Bernard Minet
* Yves Montand
* Jeanne Moreau
* Michèle Morgan
* Etienne Mélingue

N

* Philippe Noiret
* France Nuyen

O

* Pascale Ogier

P

* Herve Paillet
* Pierre Palmade
* Vanessa Paradis
* Anne Parillaud
* Gérard Philipe
* Michel Piccoli
* Roger Pierre
* Dominique Pinon
* Marie-France Pisier
* Perrette Pradier
* Yvonne Printemps
* Wojciech Pszoniak
* Jean Piat

R

* Blanche Ravalec
* Serge Reggiani
* Jean Reno
* Jean Richard
* Jean Rochefort
* Sonia Rolland
* Viviane Romance
* Benoît Régent
* Gabrielle Réjane

S

* Ludivine Sagnier
* Xavier Saint-Macary
* Maria Schneider
* Emmanuelle Seigner
* Michel Serrault
* Delphine Seyrig
* Simone Signoret
* Simone Simon

T

* Audrey Tautou
* Jean-Louis Trintignant
* Marie Trintignant
* François Truffaut

V

* Christian Vadim
* Michael Vartan
* Lino Ventura
* Hervé Villechaize
* Jacques Villeret
* Marina Vlady

W

* Anne Wiazemsky
* Lambert Wilson

Y

* Jean Yanne

APPENDIX B

THE CESAR AND MOLIERE AWARDS

The César Awards are France's most prestigious film honors. Similar to the Oscars, the winners are chosen by some 3, 000 professionals in a vote organized by the Academy of Arts and Cinema Technology (L'Académie des Arts et Techniques du Cinéma).

The Cesar Awards were first held on April 3, 1976, following the creation of the academy in 1975. The initiative to create the academy came from George Cravenne who lamented that France didn't have the equivalent of the American Oscar, and all it represents. "The Oscars, I believe, were born in 1927," he is quoted on the site saying. "I was then 13 years old, and since this age (very remote today!), I was always obsessed by the existence of this emblematic character, not of flesh and bone, but of bronze and gilding, whose reputation was planetary."

The name for the awards stem from a sculptor friend of Cravenne's, whose work inspired him to create the award for the promotion of the cinema in Europe. The first ceremony saw 13 Césars handed out, with subsequent awards created for Best Short and Best Costume. In 1983, the "most promising young actress and actor" titles were created in tribute to Romy Schneider and Patrick Deweare, and today there are some 19 different categories. Recent winners include the films L'Esquive (2003), Les Invasions barbares (2003), The Pianist (2002) and Le Fabuleux destin d'Amélie Poulain (2001).

The ceremony takes place at the end of February at one of several prestigious locations, which have included the Empire Theatre, the Salle Pleyel, the Palais des Congrès, and the Théâtre des Champs Elysée. For the 2005 ceremony, the

Academy chose the Théâtre Musical de Paris Châtelet. The ceremony has been televised on Antenne 2 for the last 18 years. Ever since the beginning, an official dinner reception is held at Fouquet's after the ceremonies, attended by artists and industry professionals.

Official website (in French): http://www. lescesarducinema. com/
Contact information
19, rue Lauriston, Paris 75116—FRANCE
Telephone 33 1 53 64 05 25

The Molière Awards are equivalent to the Tony Awards in the United States, recognizing excellence in French theatre ever since 1987, when the awards were created by A. P. A. T. (Association Professionnelle et Artistique du Théâtre). Since then, 500 personalities have been bestowed with Molière awards, with the most popular winners being Nicolas Sire, for set design (10 nominations), Stéphan Meldegg and Jean-Marie Besset, for adaptations (9 each), Jean-Marc Stéhlé, for set design (8), Jorge Lavelli, for directing (7), and Muriel Rorin, for her one woman shows. The 19th Ceremony—Nuit des Molières—was held on May 9 at the Théâtre Mogador in Paris, and was broadcast live on France 2.

Official website (in French): http://les-molieres. france2. fr/

978-0-595-67502-9
0-595-67502-6

www.ingramcontent.com/pod-product-compliance
Lightning Source LLC
Chambersburg PA
CBHW020514100426
42813CB00030B/3243/J